# THE GARDENER OF VERSAILLES

# THE GARDENER
## *of* VERSAILLES

≈≈≈≈≈≈≈≈≈≈≈≈≈≈≈≈≈≈≈≈≈≈≈≈≈≈≈≈≈≈

## MY LIFE IN
## THE WORLD'S GRANDEST GARDEN

### Alain Baraton

TRANSLATED FROM THE FRENCH BY

CHRISTOPHER BRENT MURRAY

Published in the United States of America in 2014
By Rizzoli Ex Libris, an imprint of
Rizzoli International Publications, Inc.
300 Park Avenue South
New York, NY 10010
www.rizzoliusa.com

Originally published in France as *Le Jardinier de Versailles*
Copyright © Editions Grasset & Fasquelle, 2006
Translation Copyright © 2014 Christopher Brent Murray

2014 2015 2016 2017 / 10 9 8 7 6 5 4 3 2 1

Distributed in the U.S. trade by Random House, New York
Printed in U.S.A.

ISBN-13: 978-0-8478-4268-1
Library of Congress Catalog Control Number: 2013943445

# CONTENTS
≈≈≈≈≈≈≈≈≈≈≈

# THE GARDENER OF VERSAILLES

# THE STORM
≈≈≈≈≈≈≈≈≈≈

I SLEEP LIKE a log, which is fitting for a gardener. Although I rarely suffer from insomnia (one of the privileges of my profession), the storm of December 26, 1999, was a remarkable exception. I woke up for the first time at around four in the morning. Although groggy, I could feel the walls vibrating and hear the wind whistling through the window frames. It was like being on a sailboat—the whole world seemed to split apart, to pitch, crack, and howl. I grumbled to myself that the palace wasn't going to sink and imagined the Atlantic whipped to a fury at my vacation home, on the island of Oléron. The thought calmed me back to sleep until around six, when sleeping had become impossible. The persistent noise that had been infiltrating my dreams finally woke me for good.

The Régie du Trianon, tucked in the depths of Versailles's woods, felt as though it was suspended in a state of vertigo, while outside, the whistling had given way to a low, hostile roar. I got up, but the roar was so loud that it seemed as though I was moving in silence. I had turned on the bedside lamp, walked across creaking floorboards, opening and closing doors as I went, but my actions had been put on mute, drowned out by the infernal waltz of crashing and banging outside.

I went upstairs. The room seemed to moan and struggle, caught in a battle I could never hope to influence. The individual windowpanes looked as fragile as soap bubbles. I approached but didn't dare put my face to the glass, for fear it might suddenly shatter. My thoughts turned to Marie Antoinette's oak tree, in all of its three hundred years of glory, and how it must be suffering. Then my thoughts were interrupted.

I saw trees falling, one after another, effortlessly thrown to the ground by the wind's frenzy. At first, I couldn't believe my eyes. How could these giants topple? They had already withstood so much; weren't they immortal? The strange, unreal feeling was bolstered by the fact that I couldn't hear the trees fall. Too fast, somewhat jerky, and comical—it was like watching a silent movie—to the point that I had trouble taking the scene seriously. But I knew the tumult of the wind masked the sound of the crashes. I knew there was nothing I could do, so I watched, fascinated, as dawn rose over Versailles.

At about seven, I tried to go outside with Pym, my German shepherd, but the wind was blowing so hard that it was nearly impossible to walk, even with my back against the wall, and I could hardly keep my eyes open. The phone and electricity had gone out, of course. I wanted nothing more than to take action and be of use but there was nothing to be done. I went to my office, remembering the fax that had come in the previous night warning about the approaching storm. It had been as useful then as I felt now.

The view from my office windows was terrifying. In the faint morning light, the storm had revealed the roofs of the town beyond, usually hidden behind a mass of trees. They had all been blown down. We had lost about 1,800 trees in the previous big storm of 1990. The damage was colossal, but it had allowed us to start restoring the areas of the park that had started showing their age. What I saw on that morning in December 1999 could not be described as mere damage. The park I had long loved, the park to which I owed my identity, was now dead.

Once the wind had died down, I pulled on my coat in a state of anxiety, afraid of what I would find. I felt like I'd just received a phone call bearing bad news. I wasn't alone at Versailles, but the trauma felt personal. Both restless and resigned, I tried to reason with myself: everything pointed to the worst. I braced myself and opened the door.

Outside, the air felt strangely soft and warm, but a veritable battlefield lay before me. The landscape had been upended. The bosquets, ordinarily dense and bushy, were now bare. Treetops lay on the ground. The once-geometric forms of clipped box-wood had been blown into disheveled furies.

Two young beech trees I had recently planted had been among the first to go. They were now smothered under the mass of a fallen cherry tree. My trees, once so orderly and upright, were now tangled and piled up on one another in painful chaos. They lay in agony, their roots naked and suffering, exposed to the air in a position I couldn't help but find shocking. The laws of nature, which usually seemed so clement and productive, had been swept away in a climactic upheaval that had lasted only a few hours. Another revolution had struck the subjects of Versailles, and those "subjects" (as we often refer to individual trees in French) were going to die. They had been taken away in the space of a night and there was nothing I could do about it. Deprived of the garden's protection, the palace itself suddenly seemed fragile.

Heart racing, I headed to Versailles's botanical treasure chest, the Queen's Hamlet. The surroundings had changed so dramatically that I had trouble finding my way. Nothing familiar had survived. The trees that once guided visitors through the garden were unrecognizable. Some of them lay on the ground; others had been displaced or crushed by their neighbors. Even the road was gone. In its place lay a field of mud where my boots sank to the calf. I picked through the chaos as best I could, but it was difficult going without any familiar landmarks. Here and there, twisted signs pointed absurdly to "Napoleon's Pine" or "The Queen's Allée." The kings, queens, and emperors had long disappeared from Versailles, and now the allées were gone as well. Though a few survivors remained standing, my thoughts remained riveted on Marie Antoinette's garden. Had Jussieu's cedar survived? It might have—after all, it had weathered the storm of 1990. What about the massive tulip tree? I didn't dare to even think of it. If only I could start running and calm the thoughts rushing through my head. If only I could dissolve into thin air and rematerialize directly at the entrance to the Hamlet and know what had happened! The mud and branches that had replaced the formerly beautiful allée slowed me down and I cursed the fallen trees barring the route, insulting the park I had once cherished. I had to blaze a trail and find out what had happened.

I crossed paths with one of the gardeners. He was in the same state as I, at once shattered and restless. He told me that all of the allées had been massively devastated, beyond comparison with what had happened in 1990. The garden had been disfigured. He repeated the word "disfigured," insisting on every syllable. For us, the gardens of Versailles expressed not only harmony and the pride of their creators: the grounds were also almost a person, both splendid and graceful. My colleague hadn't yet been to the Queen's Hamlet, so we decided to go there together.

We silently picked our way through the downed treetops. The allée leading to the Petit Trianon was a veritable no-man's-land. Louis XV built the Petit Trianon for Madame de Pompadour, although she never had the opportunity to enjoy it. In the end, Louis XVI gave the edifice to Marie Antoinette in celebration of his coronation. The story goes that he handed her the key in a symbolic gesture, saying, "Since you love flowers, Madame, I'm offering you a bouquet—the Petit Trianon." Although I am skeptical of this poetic utterance's authenticity, having never come across it in the archives, the sentence rings elegantly true. The Petit Trianon was a gift suitable for a beautiful woman—it is an intimate and feminine place, both brimming with artifice, and so very natural.

*"L'autrichienne"* or "the Austrian"—as Marie Antoinette was sometimes referred to in those days—disliked the official ceremonies and rigid court etiquette at Versailles. To satisfy her need for escape, Louis XVI built the Hamlet, a grouping of twelve delightful little dollhouses complete with a mill, a vegetable garden, a milking parlor, and a barn where the queen could play at being a farmer's wife. She who hated staid ceremony took refuge in the Hamlet, becoming an artificial peasant girl in a fairy-tale village.

I could make out the Tour de Malborough in the distance. Exposed and blackened as though struck by lightning, the tower had completely lost the quaint country look that had often irritated me in the past. Once fit for a princess, it had become a shadowy witch's belfry. The tower seemed so awkward and isolated in the landscape that I imagined it would give Malborough quite a shock were he to see it again.

My heart skipped a beat. At the foot of the tower, the immense tulip tree lay on its side, half-submerged in the pond. I had taken everything in so quickly and somehow not noticed it. The eye absorbs what it knows first, and I must have had no desire to register the disaster. But there it was, colossal, sinking into the duckweed like the *Titanic*. I was speechless. This hundred-foot giant, its trunk more than ten feet across, had been ripped from the ground. Beyond its immensity, the tulip tree had special historical significance. Although planted at the beginning of the nineteenth century, it was descended from the thirty-odd tulip trees that had come from Virginia under the reign of Louis XVI, during the time he supported the American Revolution.

There are many ties between Versailles and the United States. Beyond the Friends of Versailles and other charitable groups, the château has also had many generous private patrons. Just a few days after the storm, I received a call from Alexis Wittner, a friend particularly touched by the loss of the tulip tree. He offered to donate a new tree from the nurseries of the city of Atlanta where he worked. News of the lost tulip tree had circulated quite a bit on the other side of the Atlantic—this was why Hubert Astier, the president of the Domaine de Versailles, was later invited to the White House and why I was able to bring a new tulip tree to Versailles. The new tree was planted on the first day of spring by a group of students from the appropriately named Fayetteville, from which the tree had originally come.

THE STRANGEST THING about the morning after the storm was its calm. Not the slightest noise, not a single animal, just the wavelets on the pond lapping and breaking the silence at regular intervals. My tulip tree rested in peace. We bury our dead, but trees, to the contrary, are ripped from the earth. The only witnesses to the violence that had occurred the previous night were the chunks of sod that had been flung into the air as each tree crashed down, forming unsightly mounds beyond the crater left behind by the rigid, wincing roots. The notion of rigor mortis came to mind. I'm not an overly sentimental or nostalgic person; I don't wring my hands in pity over a broken vase, and I don't play Mozart for my hydrangeas. But a tree is a living thing. After living alongside my trees for more than thirty years, I've acquired more than simple know-how. I feel something like botanical sympathy; I can tell whether a tree needs attention, whether it is suffering or flourishing. The tulip tree had died before its time, and there was something tragic about that, as negligible as it was in the greater scheme of things.

The Virginia tulip tree was not the only subject to succumb to the storm. The Corsican pine had also fallen. Planted in the nineteenth century, it had attained an unusual size. Isolated and sickly in its youth, it had reminded me of a romantic hero—a Célio or Lorenzaccio—wild, shadowy, and just a little bit silly. Gone unnoticed by the Impressionists, it had nevertheless seen the likes of Corot and Utrillo who used to take pleasure in painting the gardens. Visitors used to collect its pinecones in the summer, using them to predict the weather by watching them open and close. The sugary odor of pine needles and damp was troublingly strong. The air was already starting to smell of decomposition.

Once an image of strength and majesty, the Atlas cedar had fared no better. Cedarwood is particularly weather resistant; the ancient Egyptians used cedar oil to embalm their dead. Among evergreens, the cedar seems, more than any other, to evoke survival in the face of death. Yet the wind had managed to unearth a tree whose stump alone weighed seventeen tons. Two hundred years of history disappeared along with the cedar. When Napoleon visited Versailles, he decided to fix up the Hamlet and offer it (yet again) to a woman, the Empress Marie-Louise. The gardens were redesigned and the cedar was planted on a rise just above the lake. After witnessing and weathering countless events, it was finally taken away by the storm of December 26, 1999.

I NEVER THOUGHT I would bear witness to such a dramatic spectacle. Versailles had always made me feel like I was just passing through. Not only did the trees, bosquets, and allées not belong to me, I had expected them to outlive me. Trees allow us to come to terms with a scale of time that is longer than our own. A cedar, for example, can live for up to two thousand years. The specimen that now lay at my feet was two hundred years old—a mere child.

A few survivors still stuck out in the field of ruins, breaking up the landscape and rising amid the gloomy chaos of branches, mud, and windblown thatch. It is a strangely disturbing reality that nearly every catastrophe has its survivors. Why one victim and not another? Why the precious tulip tree and not this ordinary wild cherry? The cherry tree seemed to ask the same question, surprised to be left standing. I found the situation shocking and unfair, or at least incongruous. The remaining trees seemed almost comical—erect and naked among the others reduced to brush. The survivors stuck out like guests who show up in evening wear to a casual event.

Among them, I noticed Jussieu's cedar, planted by the famous botanist Bernard de Jussieu, one of the freethinking, enlightened spirits who illuminated the eighteenth century. It didn't look its best, deprived of a good many of its supple green needles—but it had weathered the storm. When I'm inspecting the gardens and walking among the trees he once planted, I often think that I would have liked to know Jussieu. He wanted to become a pharmacist—a profession that, in those days, was closer to that of a doctor. But at university he discovered he couldn't bear the sight of blood, dashing his hopes, for bloodletting was still considered a general cure-all. Today, he would have become a psychiatrist, but much to the benefit of botanical science, psychiatry was still in the distant future. Science owes Jussieu for, among other things, creating one of the first systems used to classify plants. Versailles, a place he held particularly dear, owes many of its trees to him.

On a trip to England in 1734, Jussieu discovered the Atlas cedar and introduced the species to France. Traveling was more dangerous and slow in those times. (One can see evidence of this in the size of France's administrative regions: they were created during the Revolutionary period according to the distance a man could walk in one day.) Monsieur de Jussieu may not have traveled on foot, but he still braved many perils and had good reason to worry about both his own survival and that of his precious cedar seedling. Overburdened with baggage and anxious not to be separated from the specimen, he traveled with the tiny cedar tree hidden in his hat. Back in Paris, he managed to make it grow; today it is a good eighty feet tall and can still be admired in the center of the labyrinth of the Jardin des Plantes. The cedar at Versailles is its brother.

"All of the oldest trees are on the ground. It's a catastrophe, Alain. We'll never recover." Astier's dry, laconic tone snapped me out of my daydream. The situation was serious. Not only had he called me by my first name, he associated the two of us in his vision of the struggle ahead. Astier isn't the sort of fellow who lets himself get stuck in a boat with just anybody, unless of course it's a lifeboat. He remained irreproachably professional, as always, but a note of sadness crept into his voice as he recited the inventory of the measures taken and information gathered. He announced that the wind had blown at nearly one hundred miles per hour. The storm had formed off the coast of Newfoundland, crossed the Atlantic in under a day, and swept across all of Europe. There would be deaths. Electricity—and thus light and heat—had been knocked out in entire regions. A storm of such magnitude was virtually unheard of in Europe's temperate climate.

What would we do? There were so many decisions to be made and I didn't know where to begin. Astier felt it would be unsafe to begin work before backup support arrived, and he was right. The gardens were completely impracticable. More trees might still fall, and it was not the day to have to make a trip to the emergency room. All the roads had been cut off, and too few of us lived on-site to begin clearing up efficiently. We would also need backup equipment. I made a quick mental list: backhoes, steam shovels, dump trucks, maybe even a crane…it seemed hopeless. Versailles would be turned into a construction site. Astier reassured me that the army would send support. We would be able to count on the French state and the Friends of Versailles for aid, but according to him we would still be bankrupt. There would never be enough money to restore the gardens. I grew increasingly pessimistic. If the storm had been as bad as he claimed, if people had died, the government would do better to spend money on people instead of trees. The same was true for the town of Versailles. I should point out that the château remains a strong symbol of the ancien régime that still aggravates many; it is often the object of local envy.

I went home, obsessed with thoughts of money. We would never have enough to rebuild. I could still remember the tedious negotiations for each bag of fertilizer or seed, following the storm of 1990. The gardens have always been the poor cousin of Versailles. The château is a seat and symbol of power. No matter what regime is in place, it receives the most interest. Princes and heads of state are received, treaties are signed, and everybody senses the looming presence of Louis XIV. Money follows power the way water flows downhill. The gardens are a place of intimacy. Who would think to declare anything beyond their own love in a garden? This is probably why the gardens have always received the leftovers of Versailles's funding. In short, I knew that the storm had swept away much of the garden, but it would not change the way things had been done since the ancien régime.

An old miser's legend has it that trees sometimes hide treasures within their stumps, so later that day my children and I set out to hunt for them. All of us needed a bit of cheer and excitement after such a depressing day, but the search turned out to be gloomier than we had imagined. The children were too grown-up, I felt defeated, and the sight of so many uprooted trees only needled my pain. We were a sorry lot. Our slipping and stumbling made us laugh, but our hearts just weren't in it. None of us really believed in the old legend about treasures, but our walk had served to further convince us how extensive the damage had been, discovering only the ravages of the storm. My children were as distraught as I—they had grown up at Versailles, and the storm had taken away all of their forts and hiding places; I would now never discover them. They had lost part of their childhood, and I had lost the best twenty-three years of my life. We called it quits and went home.

A STRANGE NOISE awoke me the following morning: a fleet of helicopters landed not far from my windows. When I first heard their low, rumbling hum through my sleep, I thought it was the storm starting up again, or that I was reliving it in a nightmare. Finally, I got up to see where the horrible racket was coming from. Through the gray mist of the early morning I could make out the spinning blades whirring overhead. They were the first wave of backup support, and they had arrived with the dawn.

Astier was right about the army—I recognized the camouflage markings on the helicopters. The hour of their arrival also gave them away. Military men are extreme morning people. Any operation worthy of the name begins by six and is finished before noon, as though the twelve strokes of midday might turn their transport back into a pumpkin. Gardeners are a more reasonable lot, only getting up with the sun, which in January is never before seven in the morning.

The next miracle of the day came with the sound of the telephone ringing in my office downstairs—service had been restored! Astier was on the line, telling me to go help delegate the army contingent. Our rallying point was the Place du Grand Trianon. I had to move quickly because I knew that the number of soldiers I would have at my (and the gardens') disposal would depend on how quickly I got there. The gardens have never been a priority at Versailles, and this was no different in times of crisis. Roof tiles and windowpanes would come before my trees.

My mind raced, coming up with justifications I might use. No tourists could return to Versailles as long as the grounds remained unsafe. The debris would need to be cleared as rapidly as possible to salvage the maximum number of trees. Many had been weakened by the storm and now threatened buildings and their inhabitants. This final idea was the most promising—all of the administrators I would see that morning lived on-site with their families, as I did. If they knew that a tree was threatening to fall and smash their precious house, darling children, or luxury car, I would be certain to get as many men as I needed.

I've always had to scheme to get support for my gardens. The Versailles of today is not all that different from the Versailles described by the acid pen of the soldier, diplomat, and memoirist Louis de Rouvroy, duc de Saint-Simon: jealousy, pettiness, and intrigues, both ridiculous and tragic, still haunt the corridors of the château. Emboldened by my ruse, I dressed in a flash but took time to shave carefully. Astier, the military men, and my plans deserved the best!

It took me more than an hour to join the others. The roads were even more dangerous than on the previous day. Everywhere trees threatened to fall, landslides had been set off in the night, and the lawns had grown compacted and slippery, particularly in the heavy early morning dew. The animals that had fled in the wake of the storm had returned to their old haunts. All around me I could hear cracking branches, falling trees and debris, and other chain reactions set off by a bolting fox or pheasant. The nature that surrounded me had become unfamiliar—it felt hostile and wild. Unlike the previous day, I was a bit afraid.

In the end, my "scheme" to get as many men as possible was nothing more than a realistic description of the park. It amounted to a death wish to stroll through the gardens in their state following the storm. I arrived at the meeting, mud splattered up to my collar, looking once again like a filthy, bad-tempered gardener—a stereotyped image I hate, but at least my appearance served as testimony to my argument: the park was inaccessible to tourists and would need to be closed for several weeks. Eyes widened. I immediately understood that a few weeks' lost entrance fees were far more horrifying than the devastation of the Queen's Hamlet. All of Versailles's leading men were seated around the table: Pierre-André Lablaude, our chief architect (wearing an astonishing hat of green felt), would ultimately succeed in the daunting task of putting the park back in order. Joël Cottin, in charge of the château's gardens and bosquets, was saddened by the damage but already seemed in a mood to fight back. A bit removed from the others, Pierre Arizzoli-Clémentel, the domaine's general director, was despondent. I could see he was thinking of his château, his gardens, and especially the gardens of the Petit Trianon, which he had loved for years. Finally, I noticed the state architect, a throwback to 1900 with his thick moustache and long black coat, missing only a monocle. A few other important officials had sent their apologies for not being able to come. We needed man power and appropriate equipment to get to work immediately and reopen the park as soon as possible, in conditions that would present no danger to the public. My argument struck home—security and economy are the new magic words of French administration. I easily obtained three groups of the soldiers sent that morning.

Finally we could get down to work! In crisis, some people remain hopeless, while others are unsure where to turn and calm their anxiety in a flurry of activity. I belong to the second category and had been eager to get going since the previous day. I was unusually worked up—and for good reason: there was so much to do! With my heart pounding like a boy on a first date, I strode toward the broad lawn of the Grand Trianon where the army battalions were waiting.

The sight of the armored equipment rolling down the park's roads was disconcerting—Versailles is more often used as a set for films and events. One frequently sees fake marquesses laced into corsets walking through the gardens, or the passage of bewigged horsemen impersonating Voltaire or Valmont, according to the period and their degree of lucidity. Versailles's paradox is that everything that is contemporary feels anachronistic. As much as the palace is part of my daily life, I am continually astonished to find that it contains coffee machines and televisions; it was equally strange to see the gardens full of military equipment and soldiers in camouflage.

Imagine my surprise when I caught sight of the men: an entire battalion from France's tropical overseas territories, turning blue in the bitter December morning. The practical sense of the top brass who had sent them was clearly limited to strict matters of engineering. Numb with cold, teeth chattering, they seemed about as comfortable as France's Senegalese troops come north to fight in the trenches of the First World War. Before doing anything else, I offered everybody a round of hot coffee to bolster morale. I, who had wanted to get started clearing up straight away, found myself running an improvised tearoom in the Orangerie.

At last we got to work. In order to clear the terrain and evaluate what remained, we collected the fallen trees with hoists and trucks, and burned them in the depths of the park—an area less affected by the storm. After a few days' work it became necessary to face the truth: almost nothing was left. More than 18,000 trees had been destroyed—either uprooted on the day of the storm or so damaged that they had to be cut down. Even the soldiers—who had seen worse—seemed saddened by their work. Apart from a few specimens, including Marie Antoinette's oak, which, by some miracle, had survived the disaster, many precious trees now lay in the depths of the park, in a place whose strange, solemn atmosphere felt like a cross between a logging camp and an elephant graveyard.

There was something unreal about the week Versailles was closed: the park itself, once a treasure of order and harmony, had been turned into a vast trench, muddy, marred by gashes and mounds of earth, frequented by soldiers and machines straight out of a science-fiction movie. Modern machines—while undeniably useful—are ugly almost to the point of fascination. Sometimes I wonder whether their hideous design is intentional. The excavator takes the prize, with its ravenous articulated jaws that slowly consume the earth in a deafening racket. I never imagined Versailles could fall into such disgrace. Relatively spared by wars, the gardens had encountered their own Hiroshima. This is a gross exaggeration of course, but the defeat was such that the thought repeatedly crossed my mind.

Flashes of hope were regularly crushed by disappointment. The Bassin de Trèfle, one of my earliest accomplishments, was in ruins. When I first arrived, the *bassin* was a sort of dumping place for the usual hodgepodge of scraps found in every garden. I was given charge of the area. It was unrewarding and unappealing work—the sort of chore that always falls to the new guy. At the time I had the idea to plant a rough country lawn—the fashion of the day was still for smooth, flawless English-style lawns, but I wanted something thick and dense—the kind of grass that makes you want to run barefoot, where you might pick a few daisies before forgetting them in the depths of a pocket. I had the idea and it worked well. Since those days, country wildflower lawns have sprung up all over the place.

In my early days at Versailles I had been assigned projects in similar spots, less known to the average visitor, but which would became dear to my heart. The storm had ravaged many of them. The park and gardens were not mine to claim—nature belongs to none of us—but they were certainly my pride.

I didn't have a very easy childhood, and all my life, I've found affirmation through my work. But my work, the park, had just been taken away. My secret desire had been to take one last walk down my cherished allées on the day of my retirement and see the trees I had planted grown into solid specimens. Now that wish would never come true. I knew we would replant, of course—since the storm of 1999 we have replanted more trees at Versailles than had been planted in two centuries—but those trees don't belong to me. Those are the storm's trees.

I WAS IN such a state of disgust that I had forgotten my natural timidity. When, by chance, I was put in charge of receiving the journalists who had come to cover the story, I felt like a man on fire. Normally retiring and withdrawn, I became provocative and flamboyant—my words flowed spontaneously. I was vehement, telling how the park had been devastated, the trees blown down, France's heritage lost—and people listened. My anger had finally found a target and the microphones caught every word. Once the television stations got hold of the news, the media invaded Versailles. All of them wanted to see the gardener. My personal tragedy was broadcast on every channel. I even received a visit from the Prime Minister. The journalists made too much of it, but they gave me confidence and gave me hope. I remember one headline in particular, "The Head Gardener's Tears," in a magazine devoted to revealing the romantic escapades of Europe's last royals to common mortals. This publication usually devoted its pages to Prince Charles, not his gardener. I had, of course, not cried during the interview, but I remember feeling very touched when a frail grandmother called to say she had seen me in the magazine. For me, the post-storm media frenzy was a time of recognition, but for the park it was a miracle. Donations started flooding in and Versailles was saved.

A final incident rounded out that crazy week. The gardens of Versailles welcome anonymous hordes of tourists, but they also possess a small group of regular visitors who come to daydream, read, or go jogging, and we know them well. These regulars are part of our family, inhabiting an intermediate zone between the tourists and the people who live on the domain year-round. There are the two little old men in caps who always sit on the same bench, not speaking; the jogging woman with a pony-tail; and the moody teenager who comes to read classic novels and smoke cigarettes—not necessarily in that order. Countless stories circulate among the gardeners, and the slightest change in a regular's behavior is discussed in depth. I have alternately heard from various "reliable sources" that the two little old men are brothers, gay, and embittered socialist party activists. (One of my colleagues has already pointed out that the three hypotheses are not mutually exclusive.) The lady jogger is the source of fantasies among the men and a fair amount of jealousy among the women—the former imagining her torrid past, the latter the overly defined muscles of her "completely unfeminine" future.

The regulars break up the monotony of our days, but they are also the true lovers of Versailles. For them, the temporary closing of the park was a trauma. Many came every morning to ask if the park was going to open soon, in spite of the "Closed" sign clearly hanging from the gate. Others would call every day at the same hour to ask about the progress, like visitors checking in on a convalescing invalid.

Among the regulars, there was one whom I had dubbed "the elegant woman." She came to the park alone, without any particular reason or goal. She didn't have a book, a dog, or knitting to do, and yet she would sit on a bench for a good hour, legs crossed, back ramrod straight. She never seemed like she was meditating or thinking about anything—she was motionless. The gardens' statues sometimes seemed more lifelike. Rather pretty, she was always elegantly dressed, but always the same way, which seemed odd for somebody who at first glance seemed like a coquette: ankle boots, a narrow skirt, and a light-colored coat. We would sometimes exchange a few words. During one of those conversations she told me her name. Once, I saw the man who must have been her husband—visibly quite rich and much older—come to meet her. There was something opaque and mysterious about the woman that intrigued me. More than that, she was like a character in a novel or movie—she wouldn't have been out of place in a film noir from the 1940s, the kind where the actors wear fedoras low on their foreheads, exchanging witticisms and revolver fire, enveloped in the thick smoke swirling from their endless cigarettes. I could also imagine her in a silent movie (she had the right sort of pale complexion and ghostlike expression), the kind of movie that always gives me goose bumps even if it's a Chaplin comedy, because I can't help thinking how everybody—from the actors to the directors, cameramen, and costume makers—is long dead.

The woman had become part of my "mental novel," the one that, without having any literary pretentions, I mentally write and rewrite on a daily basis. About a week after the storm, I was told that the elegant woman had called and wanted to talk to me. She inquired after the park, and in my mind, she returned to her ordinary identity, Mrs. So-and-So, the well-heeled married woman with whom I occasionally stop to chat. During the difficult circumstances of that week, I hadn't been particularly inclined to think of the characters that populate my imagination. I told her the latest news and she asked self-consciously if it might be possible for me to show her around the park—she hadn't been to the gardens for a week and was starting to miss them. I found her request touching and accepted without a moment's hesitation. Her sadness seemed sincere, and I thought perhaps her rich husband was also generous. He might make a donation. We set an appointment for the following morning.

She arrived early—I could make out her long silhouette— standing slender and stiff at the palace gates among the gawkers and journalists. She waited with the grave immobility that seemed to be part of her personality. Instead of her usual ensembles, built around the coat of that bourgeois shade of beige whose very discretion is an outward sign of wealth, on that day, she wore a long, black coat. She told me she was in mourning for the park. I felt uncomfortable at what seemed like melodrama and was in a hurry to get the visit over with. We got into my car and I began to tell the story of the storm for the umpteenth time. I have to admit that after a week of interviews, television appearances, and administrative reports, I had grown tired of the same old speech, one to which she didn't seem to be listening. Was she nervous to be alone with me in a car? She kept pulling her coat around her knees. Her prudishness surprised me because, in my imagination at least, the "elegant woman" also had a certain amount of daring. But even though I spend most of my time in the woods, I'm no wild man—and the situation hardly lent itself to flirtation. The seriousness of my words finally seemed to allow her to relax.

Upon her request, we headed to the back of the park. I tried to convince her that this part of the grounds was of little interest because it had hardly been touched by the storm, but she remained firm. The depths of the gardens were her favorite spot, she was used to spending hours there, and she was counting on my generosity. I politely obeyed and told myself it would give me a chance to inspect the area. When we arrived I was glad to see that my men had done their jobs, and the few fallen trees were now cleared away. The elegant woman had returned to her usual silence, her serious gaze fixed upon the landscape. I waited for a good ten minutes without breaking that silence, thinking that it couldn't be easy to spend every day with such a quiet person. I decided to smoke while she contemplated. My back turned, I plunged my head inside my coat to create a shelter from the wind where I could light my cigarette. Imagine my surprise when I turned around to see the elegant woman standing stark naked, her long coat around her feet. She looked straight into my eyes without speaking a word. Her gaze was at once mystic and threatening, like the women in paintings by Gustave Moreau. But this Salomé said nothing: she was very beautiful, and nobody would have interrupted us, but cold beauty has never captured my imagination, even after a storm. Most of all, I didn't want my mental novel to become a drugstore romance. The difficult thing, I realized, would be to avoid making her feel ridiculous— the most mortifying and even insulting result of this kind of situation. Silent and solemn, I picked up her coat and placed it respectfully around her shoulders. We said nothing further and I drove her back to the gates. She shook my hand as though nothing had happened and we parted ways. A few days later, I learned that her husband had made a rather generous donation.

I remain perplexed as to her motivations. Had she wanted to fulfill a fantasy and put some spice into a boring life, or had the death of the park given her the desire to make love? Of course, I can never know, but the story, beyond flattering me, shows how the park is a place where the unexpected, and even the extraordinary, can happen at any moment. It may seem naive, but for me, the gardens of Versailles are enchanted. They are more than a witness of France's history: they contain thousands of intimate stories that my almost forty years in their company have taught me to better understand. This is the private, personal side of Versailles that I want to share. A great deal has been written about the château and much less about the gardens, but always in the same, biased manner. Too many books sanctify or vilify Versailles. Both tendencies are unfair and lack nuance. I've watched the park evolve since 1976—weathering heat, cold, and drought; I've seen it age and be born again, rising from the ashes before almost dying in the storm of 1999. Today, thanks to that same storm, I've acquired a voice, and it's a voice that I'd like to use in the service of the gardens that I love, the gardens that have made me who I am.

# APPRENTICESHIPS

≈≈≈≈≈≈≈≈≈≈≈≈≈≈≈≈≈≈≈

AT SOME POINT in my childhood, I was nicknamed "Cow Pie." Although I would remain Cow Pie to my six brothers and sisters, I fought back, and my earliest concentrated efforts of imagination were dedicated to finding equally dignified monikers for them. Even though they didn't always call me by that name, it was worse to know that I was also Cow Pie to my parents. I was a son who was neither good nor bad and who would never amount to much. You won't hear me telling fond, nostalgic stories about my youth, and if there is a period in my life upon which I turned the page without regrets, it would definitely be my childhood.

The fifth in a family of seven children, I was not born under a lucky star. Parents usually prefer their older children. And if the younger brother often triumphs in fairy tales, in real life he is usually met with indifference, receiving neither attention, nor kindness, nor much of anything at all. I was no exception to this rule; I was neither the first nor the last and my grades in school were just as middling—as far from the leader of the class as from the dunce's inexplicable prestige. My parents didn't know what to do with me—I wasn't an intellectual, but I didn't seem fit to be a laborer. This may be the reason I became a gardener—a profession defined more by a place than by any one particular activity. But at the risk of disappointing some, I have to admit that I never thought I would grow up to be a gardener. I didn't imagine becoming anything when I was a teenager. To a certain extent, I still wonder what I want to do with my life today. When I was sixteen, I took up photography as a hobby. The equipment put a serious strain on my limited budget and I started working as a gardener to be able to pay for my first reflex camera. During that summer, I rode down the country roads west of Paris on an old motorized bike that had once belonged to my mother. More bike than motor, it never went uphill without stalling. I mowed, weeded gardens, and watered lawns for pay when neighbors were on vacation. I didn't especially enjoy the work, but what else was I to do? I was too shy and immature to have worked as a clerk or a waiter—I would have never dared to approach the clients, particularly the women. My mother had dismissed the possibility of babysitting, repeating one of her favorite phrases, "If we squeezed your nose, my boy, milk would still come out." In other words, I was no figure of virile authority. Those words may have seemed harmless to her, but they stung in my memory long afterward. I never fought back or tried to change the harmless role in which my family so enjoyed casting me—preferring instead to just accentuate it. To the point that when I received my first driving license, I handed the clerk behind the counter the only photo I had of myself—taken when I was exactly thirteen years old. Never a rebel, I was at most a joker. This is the reason that my parents finally gave up and enrolled me in horticultural school. I didn't resist, but I never had what others refer to as "a calling."

My parents were of a generation and class where one didn't choose whether to have children. Ours was an old-fashioned Catholic family, and in the 1950s, children just arrived "by chance," always at the worst moment. I don't think my mother wanted to have so many children. I remember the day I discovered a photo of her in her youth—smiling, in a summer dress— happy in a way I had never seen her. She had been very beautiful—the essence of beauty—but maybe all little boys think their mothers are beautiful. At any rate, she certainly seemed to have expected a different sort of life when she married my father, a dashing man with a decent job. But the payments on our house soon ate up all of my father's resources and there was nothing left at the end of the month to pay for any extras. My mother came from a humble background and had never dreamed of Ferraris or vacations in Chamonix, but I think she would have liked to be able to stop counting pennies, pregnancies, and the passing years. Instead of champagne and roses, she found herself in a tiny suburban house paid for with every last franc, burdened with seven children who had stolen her youth, and an aging husband born before the First World War. Looking back, it's hard to reproach her for a lack of motherly love. When I see young mothers in awe of their offspring, cuddling their babies and covering them in kisses, I always think back to how I never knew my mother's touch, how I never held her in my arms, even on the day that my father died. She was never tender toward her children or toward herself. Unlike for her, life has given me the opportunity to stop and take notice. In spite of it all, I will always be indebted to her for bringing me into the world.

I still love photography. When I think back to my adolescence, it's the images that come first—the story of my family is a photo album. I always imagine my father the same way: a straight-backed little man, polite and elegant, a mix between the French actor Pierre Fresnay and Fred Astaire. The son of a successful engineer trained at the prestigious Ecole Polytechnique, he had a martial air about him, even when he left the house in the morning to do his rounds as an inspector for the French welfare system. We were never close. There was a generation gap, of course: my father was born in 1912 and was already forty-five by the time I came along. In even my earliest memories he is already an aging man. In later years he was always extremely distant. Out of stupid social convention, he required that we use the formal *vous* instead of the more familiar *tu*—I think it was Fresnay, in fact, who says in one of his movies, "I say *vous* to my father and my wife." It was already old-fashioned and vaguely ridiculous to do so in the 1940s—but ten years after the student uprisings and social shifts of May 1968, the formal *vous* was still the law with which Jacques Baraton reigned over his family.

I will admit, however, that we did live much closer to bourgeois Versailles than to the leftist hotbed of Nanterre farther to the north. My father regularly waxed rhapsodic over "his" successful son, a mathematician who took great pleasure in torturing my sisters and me with his success—such is the prerogative of older children. I was not spared any of childhood's frustrations, from the short pants and heavy shoes that I was made to wear until the age of sixteen, to a painful and useless set of braces. My true birth happened at Versailles, on a very hot day in 1976—and my real family is the one that I created over the following years in the shade of the gardens where I put down roots.

In the gray memories of my slug-like youth, a single figure remains haloed in a benevolent glow: my grandfather and his garden in Celle-Saint-Cloud, my childhood Eden. Going to my grandparents' house was always a treat. If my memories of their long-gone, ramshackle, little wood-frame house are cloudy, I can still distinctly see the garden that was my grandfather's pride. There was a small iron gate, two round flower beds that I used to admire, the clematis clambering over its pergola, and the magnificent *potager* where my grandfather grew rows of leeks standing at attention and heads of lettuce the taste of which supposedly had a hint of hazelnut. There was also a cherry tree and a magnificent damson plum. I owe my earliest romantic successes to that plum tree. During the summer, I would take my conquests to pick plums and steal a kiss instead. Gardens lend themselves to romance, and after more than thirty years as a gardener, I'm even convinced that a garden's capacity for inspiring romance should be a criterion for evaluation in terms of horticultural excellence. A garden capable of attracting lovers is a success. Who would declare their love in the arid, monotonous monochrome of the Tuileries, where it feels as though one is under perpetual surveillance? To me, this is the antithesis of a beautiful garden.

Versailles is packed with couples looking to shelter their affairs within a grove of trees, and when I see these couples, I experience professional satisfaction, not tenderness. The park's guards however, pursue them with childish, sadistic delight. In a way, the hunt for romantic couples has replaced the hunt for wild game—I must admit I greatly prefer the substitution. Sometimes the guards will call us to show off a catch. I always answer their calls to make sure that the situation isn't too seedy or tragic, but also because the story is often rather amusing. A few years ago, security called, extending a stern invitation to help them "clean up" the lawn behind the Grand Trianon. We discreetly made our way to the spot where two teenagers were engaged in an act that was quite visibly new to them. Settled down just behind the central allée on the broad lawn leading to the Gally Farm, they had chosen a poor spot. The young man was applying himself in a clumsy, gulping motion between the young woman's legs. The guard blew his whistle and the young man raised his head, just as the girl, in a natural reflex, snapped her knees together, nearly strangling her lover. I could barely breathe I was laughing so hard. The guards chased them off, of course, but I was proud to know that my park had served as their Garden of Eden.

But back to my first garden, the foundation of so much that would later become important to me—or rather, back to its creator, my grandfather. I'm not well informed about the psychological reasoning behind the rule—something I voluntarily leave to the experts—but generally, if you detest your parents and find them clichéd and conventional, you only have to jump a generation for conformity to become reassuring. The more your grandfather is the very picture of a grandfather, the more your devotion to the man is boundless. Mine was the essence of a grandfather beyond reason—a drippy nose, knee-high boots, a blue apron, a straw hat, and a pair of pruning shears always in hand. He was a model gardener that, out of respect (or fear of ridicule), I refuse to become.

Émile Crochard did not have an easy life. Born to unknown parents, he had been adopted by a couple of Belgian carnival workers and was selling gingerbread in itinerant village fairs before he even knew how to read. (I hate carnivals—I find them sad and vulgar.) The Second World War left him with a severe hand injury (all of the tendons cut) and an extreme hatred of Germans. I can still see him, his right hand prudishly folded out of sight, the dead branch of his ancient body. I'm not sure how he became a violin maker, but I know that when he was too old to work anymore, the same boss who had taught him his trade gave him only a day's salary to serve as his retirement fund. The need to put food on the table, in the very simplest sense of the phrase, brought about the birth of his model garden. The cut flowers and clematis came later.

Today our gardens, and Versailles was a precursor in this sense, are largely ornamental ones—extra rooms built outside the home. We furnish them with lounging chairs and barbecues, or even a swimming pool. The vegetable garden, if one exists, is largely there to allow the lady of the house to play farmer like Marie Antoinette before her. If she has any concerns about her potatoes and carrots, or more frequently, her cherry tomatoes (more stylish, expensive, and less nourishing—the very epitome of useless food), it's more out of pride than the fear of not being able to feed her family. This type of gardener is proud of having planted a "kiwi-tree" on the balcony of her two-room Parisian apartment. I promise to hang myself from that supposed kiwi-tree if it survives its new owner! None of this is reprehensible or even regrettable and I wouldn't want anybody to suffer a food shortage. But a good gardener should never lose sight of the fact that gardening is a perpetual balancing act of pleasure and necessity. The healthiest plants are obtained by those who know and respect the laws of nature. This was how La Quintinie, one of Louis XIV's master gardeners, succeeded in growing orange trees at Versailles without having to move them inside for the winter—something which is usually necessary in the climate of northern France. To protect his trees from the cold, La Quintinie surrounded them with little cages of wood and glass. To give them the sunshine necessary for fruit to develop he invented miniature greenhouses. If, to satisfy a royal caprice, a master gardener managed to overcome the laws of nature, it was because he understood them so well.

I have long tried, in vain, to rediscover the variety of clematis that once grew in my grandfather's garden. He died too soon for me to be able to tell him how much I admired him, how much I feel indebted to him. He never called me Cow Pie, and even though he didn't have the time to teach me all of the things he knew, he had a real passion for what would later become my life's work. I wanted him to be proud of me because I was proud of him. He was an extremely peaceful man, who knew how to show his authority without ever raising his voice—and he needed that authority when faced with my thundering grandmother who unflinchingly slaughtered chickens and rabbits. My sister and I had secretly nicknamed her "Big Bertha." She once gave us a baby chick that we named Fifi, as we did all of our pets. Six months later, Fifi ended up on our dinner plates, cooked with loving care by my triumphant grandmother. She was tough in the way peasant women are, just as my grandfather was gentle the way I like to think that gardeners are. A charming man, he indirectly passed his interests on to me. Even though he never openly encouraged me to become a gardener—he was too gentle to tell people what they should do—he showed me the way. In short, he understood me before I did. When I feel proud about what I'm doing today, it's in thinking back to him.

After the big storm, I was given all sorts of awards: Chevalier, and then Officer of Agricultural Merit, Chevalier of the National Order of Merit, Chevalier of Arts and Letters, the Silver Medal of the Society of Sciences and Encouragment…At present, I have more decorations than a Christmas tree. It seems that I have become part of the Republic's aristocracy, and at every official ceremony, I think of Émile Crochard, who struggled and suffered so much for France, and who well deserved a medal. These signs of official respect are incidental, in my eyes, mostly due to the circumstances in which I found myself rather than my merit. Still, there is one award I hope to eventually receive: the Legion of Honor—if only because it comes with an acceptance speech. There I would have a worthy forum for honoring the memory of all of those honest, talented, and underappreciated gardeners, beginning with my grandfather. He died when I was hardly out of horticulture school, and I would have loved for him to know me as a gardener. For now, may these pages stand in homage to him.

My years at horticulture school in Le Tremblay-sur-Mauldre were not the grand liberation you might expect—quite the opposite. Until then, I had been shy, anxious, and a bit slow. Away at boarding school, I was simply miserable. I didn't pay attention in class, apart from the class of Monsieur Cazot, who forced us to learn the Latin names of plants by heart—providing a means of finally seeming intellectual when I returned home to see my much-longed-for parents on Fridays. Monday mornings were particularly difficult. All of my schoolmates told stories about their weekends' sexual exploits—which I later learned were entirely fabricated—while, sheepishly, I carefully hung my week's worth of shirts, their clean smell reminding me of home and my mother.

Living with three hundred other teenage boys is no easy affair—especially if you're on the scrawny side. Although I eventually grew out of it, at seventeen I was the very essence of a runt—to the point that my homeroom teacher regularly made the easy play on words, "Baraton but not *baraqué*." (*Baraqué* is the French equivalent of "brawny.") How can one be expected to respect authority after an experience like that? Boarding school and my late teens are probably the part of my life that I look back on and understand the least. For some, it's a fun, careless time of life, but for me it was nothing at all. There were the usual rites of adolescence, of course, and in that department I didn't miss out on anything—from stealing the hall monitor's keys and sneaking out at night to the dirty handkerchiefs we called "SM's" for *spécial masturbation*, which I put with the rest of the wash, with the sniff of a feigned runny nose, in front of my mother, who believed (or mercifully pretended to believe) that I had a perpetual cold. The inventor of Kleenex has since comforted, among other things, the guilty consciences of countless teenaged boys. Those years probably had their importance, but they seem so insignificant today, so flat and banal, that they now leave me utterly indifferent.

At the end of three years of study I received, somewhat in spite of myself, two diplomas, neither of which corresponded to the then-prestigious French *baccalauréat*, which allows its recipients to attend universities. In those days, not having the "*bac*" was hardly unheard-of—in fact, it was much more common to not have one. My youth was riddled with humiliations, but a missing diploma is not one of them. French celebrities who go on about their difficult childhoods and put on acts to confess that they never got their *bacs* make me smile on the rare occasion they don't simply annoy me. Back then, it was still possible to get an education and be promoted to a job in public service without the *bac*—with a bit of hard work, one could still build a career. Today, the same students have to make it through a gauntlet of special institutions with pretentious names and obtain equally grandiose-sounding diplomas before they can start showing what they are capable of. What the system lacks in developing modesty it compensates with by developing patience. The career that I started at the end of the 1970s would now be out of reach for somebody with the profile I had at the time. To become a *chef de travaux d'art*—or to put it more simply, to have my job—one now has to have degrees from a system of prestigious schools that I can't be bothered to understand.

During the summer of 1976, the weather was beautiful and extraordinarily hot. I was hungry for freedom and independence—in other words, a motor scooter that would allow me to get away from the house. I had to find work. Versailles was the regional capital and known for its gardens, and it sat proudly just down the hill from Celle-Saint-Cloud (my motorized bike was in its death throes). Gide wrote that one should always follow their path, as long as it keeps climbing upwards, but I challenge you to climb anything with a broken *vélomoteur*! Coasting down the slope, I arrived happy and proud on the Grande Esplanade, one of the broad avenues that lead to the palace. I was as stirred up as if I had just discovered America. It was the first day of my adult life—heady and delicious.

What mysterious force led me to the director's office? A more conceited person might say it was destiny, but I remember asking for directions from a guard who responded in a Corsican accent so thick that I understood nothing. I wandered aimlessly for the next forty-five minutes, sweating and anxious, through the château's labyrinth of corridors before coming across a door that seemed larger and more ornate than the others. More importantly, it was open.

The room was bathed in light, yet cool in spite of the summer heat. It bore all of the outward signs of pomp and importance—from the old masters hanging on the walls to the shelves of rare books and armchairs as deep as tombs, to the gilded moldings and massive chandelier. I hardly noticed any of it, petrified by the gaze of the man seated across from me. With his sweep of silver hair, steely gaze, gold cane, and signet ring, Gérald Van der Kemp was so lordly that it felt only natural when he addressed me as "young man," so stone-faced that he was often portrayed as a sculpture. His name alone was intimidating: Van der Kamp, known to others as VDK.

I didn't know it then, but he was a world-renowned art expert. He arrived at Versailles after the Second World War and had worked with many great men—de Gaulle, Malraux,

Rockefeller—putting a shine unmatched since the Revolution on a château that had been in decline when he found it. Anybody who knows something about the history of Versailles knows that Van der Kamp was responsible for restoring the Queen's Grand Apartment as well as bringing back important pieces of furniture that had been scattered throughout various French ministries, including the King's Desk, a masterpiece of eighteenth-century craftsmanship. Restoring the château to its former splendor might seem like an obvious goal today, but it was the labor of Van der Kamp's entire life. Reweaving the silk brocades that cover the walls of the royal bedrooms took twenty-five years for the Queen's Bedroom and thirty for the King's Bedroom. The patterns were so complex and the materials so precious that the silk-weavers of Lyon could only produce three centimeters of fabric a day. Van der Kamp had to continually seek funding and fight for Versailles—the idea of cultural heritage and, more importantly, the need for integrity, was just emerging.

But I knew nothing of all this when I arrived in his office. I felt ridiculous and weak, blushing when he asked me what I wanted. Quivering, I stammered who I was. Van der Kamp rose from his chair and took me to see the head of the guards who was looking for seasonal workers.

He led me down to the grand statue-lined staircase under the astonished gaze of one of his underlings—normally nobody could just walk into Van der Kamp's office as I had done—callers had to pass through several circles of belligerent secretaries and inquisitive guards. I still wonder how I was able to slip past the surveillance of so much personnel! For once, I had been lucky. At any rate, it was nothing I had planned.

I walked across the empty courtyard under the crushing heat—the height of summer had dried up the grass as well as the tourists—and entered a dark and dirty office with low ceilings. The complete antithesis of the place I had just left, it was a dusty hole that needed airing out. Nothing decorated its graying walls apart from an impressive number of empty bottles and a motley gallery of objects unified by their common filth and uselessness. This is the first time I realized that the Versailles of the gardens is truly the opposite of the Versailles of the château. I then had the honor of meeting the inimitable, unerring, and irreplaceable Monsieur Chock. In those days, the directors were military men and the magnificent Monsieur Chock prided himself on being an *adjudant-chef*. As round and jolly as VDK was lean and distant, he immediately made me feel comfortable. I had trouble keeping myself from laughing when he donned a kepi that was visibly three sizes too small for his huge, bulging head, before struggling into a uniform jacket that was far too small for his broad shoulders and prominent belly. Between this little man with his hat like a cigarette butt and the stately Van der Kamp, I had truly encountered two different sides of France.

Chock hired me as a ticket seller and took me to the place that would, starting the following morning, become my place of work. We were quite the couple, him on a motor scooter that

threatened to collapse under his rotund silhouette, and me following behind, pedaling like mad on my VéloSolex, which, caught
up by the excitement of it all, had refused to start. We were so
unimpressive that the few tourists who had braved the heat barely
stood aside to let us pass. Chock nearly ran down a group from
Japan, shouting, *"Place, place!"* before roundly cursing them.

Tourism was different in those days. There were simply far
fewer foreign visitors, because visas and plane tickets were quite
expensive. Their rarity made foreigners seem more rich and
exotic. They were quite a contrast to the average French visitors
to the park—small families who had come to picnic on the lawns
with transistor radios and some sandwiches.

We finally made it to the abominable huts where I would
work for an entire summer. Probably guard posts recuperated
from some embassy and hastily repainted green to cover the
original colors of the French flag, the rotting wooden ticket
stands stood at the entrance to the park and served as a sort of
tollbooth for the cars that were still allowed to drive around the
grounds. How could they have tolerated something so ugly at the
palace gates? I understand when I think how much the new, far
more attractive stands that were installed a few years ago cost.
Much has changed at Versailles. If the park seems better maintained than it used to be, it's above all else because the budget for
maintenance has nearly doubled in less than fifteen years.

Those who worked the ticket stands were a motley crew.
There was a Spaniard, a notorious alcoholic, who insulted visitors

who didn't have exact change. He arrived every morning with his parrot's cage strapped to the back of his motor scooter—he and his bird never parted company. His religious devotion to his pet was a sign of the gentle nature that lay (as is so often the case) beneath his rough exterior. The parrot squawked all day, and his booth reeked of bird droppings and cheap wine. Then there was the colleague whose uniform was always impeccable. In spite of his dignified, military air, he turned out to be a small-time crook. Probably due to his intransigent appearance, he had been trusted with the task of distributing tickets to the cars as they arrived. One day, he dropped his book of ticket stubs, and when I stooped to pick it up, I noticed that the numbers on the tickets weren't consecutive. Standing ramrod straight, he explained in a clipped accent that he liked for everything to be tidy. He ironed the tickets when he ironed his shirts. Freshly pressed, the old tickets were "like new" and the profits could easily be slipped into the starched pockets of his jacket. He added, teasing, that my own uniform was rarely presentable. Stunned, I realized that I was honest after all. There was also a retired agent from the riot police, who liked to keep the parrot company and reminisce about his lost authority. And there was the drunk. He always scared me with his pale, watery eyes and bright red face. I couldn't tell you what his voice sounded like—I rarely heard him speak, apart from cursing his wife under his breath. His other half was a matron as thoroughly gin soaked as he—he beat her, but not, I think, without her putting up a considerable fight. Some people even said that he sold her body for drink, but it was hard to imagine who would have wanted her. I was still young, but they soon swept away any remaining illusions I might have had about romance—they were sordid, comic, and sad. The drunkard's wife represented, for me, the very image of degradation. Had she once been beautiful? She was so wracked by the effects of drink that one could no longer even guess. I'm no partisan of prohibition; to the contrary, I even planted vineyards at Versailles. But alcoholism, a common problem among gardeners, horrifies me. They were a couple straight out of Zola, and I don't much like Zola. (Not that I have a particularly developed literary sense, but I find his style heavy.) Perhaps I've always had a taste for regularity and logic. Is it the taste of Versailles?

The drunk didn't last the summer. One morning his car was found in the Grand Canal—inebriated as usual, he had driven right into the water. My coworkers joked about it, saying that he had never had much use for water, but some of them were sad, and I think we also felt a twinge of guilt. I was personally appalled by the whole grotesque story. The thing that got to me was not that he had died a fool but that he had died so foolishly. Every year, a group on the Internet attributes the Darwin Awards to the stupidest deaths, and one of my greatest fears is to be a recipient. Upon returning to France from a recent trip to China, a violent storm greeted our arrival. The sky was full of lightning and the plane shook so hard it seemed it might fall apart. I had the great luck to fly first class, and as a consequence, I had received a pair of comfortable white bedroom slippers that were supposed to help make the eleven-hour flight more tolerable. Just as the plane was going into its landing pattern, I put my shoes back on. My neighbor, visibly an experienced flyer with the confident air of a man who knows what he's talking about, told me that, given the weather, we wouldn't be on the ground for another half hour. I was tempted to retort that if we were going to crash at the end of the runway, I didn't want my cadaver to appear in slippers in the pages of *Paris Match*. The faces of the dead are traditionally embalmed wearing a false, triumphant smile. I have no problem with artifice—it is one of the principal tools of my trade—it's the smile that gets me. Without going overboard in the department of dying wishes, my only request would be that I keep my dignity.

My arrival at Versailles was almost forty years ago, but it was a very different France then, or at least, a different Versailles. We were still in the postwar world. Most of my coworkers had been hired after the war and were finishing their careers (people tend to stay on in Versailles, a stability that seems archaic today). Versailles is already a provincial place and a town with a certain nostalgia for the past. It was natural for it to be out of sync not only with Paris, but with the rest of contemporary life. Hints of another time still survive at Versailles. When I see our polite, civilized personnel and consider the huge number of regulations and other recommendations that they are expected to uphold and respect, I remember with astonishment and a bit of sentimentality the Versailles of my youth. It was like something out of a film by Tati: cars driving in whatever direction they liked; people honking their horns; and to keep the order, two armed policemen on motorcycles, who drove on the lawns and raced each other down the allées in the evenings. One of them was Indian and only took off his turban to put on his helmet. He liked to use his revolver and had taken to firing shots in the air to enforce the "keep off the grass" signs. At some point he must have been told that even firing into the air could be dangerous and that it was better to use his whistle. Thereafter, he would begin by giving a short tweet on his whistle, leaving enough time for the rest of us to come running and watch our favorite motor cop clearing the lawns in the style he preferred, with triumphant joy. These days the administration is far more serious: there are no more police officers on motorcycles and nobody carries a firearm.

The other personnel were no less colorful. I remember a certain Monsieur Alexandre, a gardener by trade, but physically, a Hercules. He was so strong that he could lift by himself the cash registers it took two or three of us to move. A man of few words, it was clear that he was not to be dallied with. One day, when he was nearly sixty, a visitor to the park pushed his luck. A child was playing with a ball, and, inspired by the reliable instinct of error, kicked it directly into the giant's shin. Hercules would have remained calm if the father, the very personification of the entitled native of Versailles, hadn't come and demanded an explanation, and worse, an apology. The conversation became heated. On the verge of exploding, the father launched into a speech: "My fellow, if you weren't an old man, I'd have half a mind to slap you…" He received a right hook that, much to the delight of his son, laid him flat on the ground.

In the isolated, fantastic world of Versailles, I felt like a king. It was the sort of triumphant summer where the heat is as relentless as one's confidence. The Bee Gees had just crossed the Atlantic and were singing "Holiday"; Alain Delon and Jean-Paul Belmondo were the epitome of a society that thought it was free. I too had the impression I was finally tasting that independence. A careless feeling was in the air—all punishments seemed like they might be abolished, even the death penalty. The only terrorists anybody was worrying about were Breton separatists. A bomb went off in the south wing of the palace, destroying three halls in the Galerie du Consulat, which had been inaugurated by the president only two weeks earlier. Nobody died, only one guard was injured, and yet, in those days when there was so little terrorism, people spoke of a "vision of war" and an "outrage." The media referred to the guilty parties as "carrion" and President Giscard d'Estaing made them disappear after the "attack" on Versailles as though he had only to brush them away.

By then I was riding down the hill and back up again without any problem, proud of the new Peugeot 103 moped that had finally liberated me from my mother's VéloSolex. Every evening, I drove up the hill to Celle-Saint-Cloud with the bags of money from the cash registers. This was also the sign of another age—today, armored cars take the receipts from the registers and place them in a strongbox every evening. In 1976, I carried it down the country roads of the Yvelines; the louder the change jingled, the happier I felt. Sometimes I would stop at the Parly II shopping center to buy magazines and would take out a bundle of bills to impress the salesgirl. That summer, believe me, I felt as happy as a king.

I only worked at the cash registers for three months. Choron, the head gardener, regularly came to supervise. No detail of the park's administration escaped Choron's notice. If a problem occurred, he was there within five minutes—the source of his one of his nicknames, "Zorro." The other, "Nœu-nœil" referred to his glass eye. A glass eye is rarely pleasing to behold, but when it's poorly made, it becomes downright ridiculous. Choron was extremely kind and always put on the jovial air of a true Frenchman, down to the beret, but his entire being exuded sorrow. Injured during the war, he had never been able to have children—part of the reason, I think, that he took such a liking to me. The gardens were his entire life—two years after retiring, he hung himself. There grew between us a sort of silent under-standing that made me truly happy to see him. In the course of one of our brief conversations (they rarely lasted longer than five minutes), Choron learned that I had been to horticultural school. A few days later, he offered me a job as a gardener at Versailles, starting in September. To tell the truth, I wasn't thrilled at the idea. I didn't like myself very much; I hardly had an existence of my own and was part of a generation that felt little enthusiasm for the future in general (the "*bof* generation"). That may even be how I responded to Choron's offer: with an unenthusiastic "bof"...Then he dangled the possibility of my own housing in the park and my face lit up. I would finally be able to escape my parents' authority and the constant attempts to hide my late-night returns home. I accepted his offer and my life truly began.

# ON THE PALACE STEPS

≈≈≈≈≈≈≈≈≈≈≈≈≈≈≈≈≈≈≈≈≈≈

ALTHOUGH I DON'T remember much about my first day, a few important events marked what I would call my first steps as a gardener. The park in those days was very different, down to the gardening techniques. It was old, densely planted with mature trees, and as a consequence, rather dark. All pruning was done by hand and it was often irregular. The allées were little more than dirt roads, and for want of personnel, sometimes felt abandoned. The machinery can't be compared with today's elegant equipment—it had come from the warehouses of the Ministry of Agriculture or the army. Much of it was rebuilt—we still had a vintage truck that started with a hand crank and evinced unpredictable behavior that sometimes occasioned worry; and we had a gigantic and completely uncontrollable rototiller. This rustic farm equipment fell well outside today's safety standards, but nobody gave it any thought, and there weren't any accidents. The parterres were simple, always planted in begonias, salvia, and verbena. As a whole, the gardens were extraordinarily calm and full of outdated, old-fashioned charm. I learned the basics under Choron's guidance, and he periodically checked on me to make sure everything was fine. He truly was a great man: in the pantheon of figures who helped me to find myself, there are my grandfather, the chilly Mr. Van der Kamp, and Mr. Choron with his glass eye.

Still, my true mentor was, without a doubt, Jean-Louis Salomon. With his blue overalls, Clark Gable moustache, and round belly, he looked more like a cook than a gardener. In a park as huge as Versailles, the gardener is more of a construction site supervisor. He speaks as often of building and transport as he does of begonias and rose gardens, and he doesn't hesitate to use force to solve problems. My first meeting with Salomon was one of the funniest. Choron had asked me if I knew how to drive a tractor, and, of course, I had lied and said I did. No sooner had I shaken his calloused hand than Salomon showed me what I would be responsible for: an enormous smoking and belching machine. I clarified that I wasn't very experienced, all the while reassuring him that I had my license for operating heavy equipment. Salomon smiled (at least, I saw the cigar he had permanently clamped between his lips rise). I think he understood. For him, from that day onward, I was one of his own, and without the slightest hint of scorn, he took pleasure in showing me how things worked. Pruning roots, watering, choosing a spot for planting in accordance with its drainage and the sort of tree to be planted—he taught me everything, the little tricks of the trade, discipline, and above all else, organization. You need to be organized if you're going to plant a bed of thirty thousand plants once, let alone every year! More than all that, it was Salomon who showed me how much gardening was about working as part of a team. He was a leader who knew how to command without sounding authoritarian, how to delegate work without seeming condescending.

Little by little, I began to notice that not only was I not so bad at gardening, but also that I liked it. I remember, in particular, the first tree that I had to replant. Some of the trees in the nursery had grown too large and had to be transplanted a kilometer away in the Bosquet des Quinconces. I can still see myself, fifteen feet off the ground in the tractor bucket, my arms wrapped around the massive trunk of the tree like a mother clutching her child. Luckily, I was up too high for people to see my face, because I suspect that my stern, concerned expression was rather amusing. Mine was a personal victory: a few years earlier, in horticulture school, I wouldn't have been capable of even moving the trunk. Back then I was "Baraton but not *baraqué*"—but now I felt like a new man and it was Salomon who gave me my new nickname. Among the various faults my parents blessed me with were my early baldness, crooked teeth, drooping shoulders, and slow mind. My parents were persuaded (and tried to persuade me as well) that they had given birth to an invalid. Among other medical devices, I had extremely painful braces. I also developed the habit of walking with my feet turned out like a duck. My brothers and sisters liked to make fun of this, but Salomon called me *"Rabat la rosée"* or "Dew-Flattener." My odd gait had the merit of evening out the grass, particularly when it was wet. At home I was the "Cow Pie," but at Versailles I became "*Rabat la rosée.*" Versailles changed me, charmed me, and appealed to me: it turned me into a man.

An important event has forever been linked with memories of my apprenticeship. Romantic and personal, it was also tied to my work. As my personal life went, it was a difficult period. I still had a lot of hang-ups and was more shy than ever, but I wanted to be attractive and my knowledge in the domain of romance was rather limited. Imagine my excitement, on that September morning when I noticed, on the north parterre, a young woman of about twenty. She had medium-long and wavy dark hair, wore a brown T-shirt, and—the height of my fantasies in those days—wasn't wearing a bra. I contemplated my muse and our eyes met—leading me to stay on at Versailles for years afterwards. It's not that I thought I would see her again, but strangely, at the moment we looked at each other, and for the first time, I felt I was in my place. Her gaze attached me to the gardens for years to come. For the first time, a woman seemed to admire me. Versailles gave me the recognition that I had always so painfully lacked. She marked me for life; today I'm still sure that I could immediately pick her out of a hundred photos.

In those days I was going through the early symptoms of a silent and creeping malady I like to call "Versailles Syndrome." There is nothing insignificant about living in Versailles—it's a real privilege. Add to this the satisfaction of being housed by the state, and often in conditions that would make a minister blush.

The French adore special privileges and the possibility of living in royal quarters without having any living costs has whetted the appetite of many a man. I know people who have taken jobs just to live in an apartment with antique moldings and bathroom fixtures. With time, the place takes hold of you and simple interest transforms itself into a passion. A passion for the place leads to a passion for its history, then for its prestige, and finally, for the power that prestige might give you. The damage begins here. The early signs are a loss of perspective that leads the afflicted to believe that Versailles is the center of the world. He lives in a sort of ideal, aristocratic community to which he has the luck of belonging. Soon the feeling of belonging to an elite group causes a violent swelling of the ego wherein the victim believes he has been invested with a mission, accompanied with an abusive use of the royal "we." The patient takes to speaking of the king, more specifically, of Louis XIV, in the present tense (female patients are more inclined to rave about Marie Antoinette). The subject is victim to attacks of dementia that lead him to wear the fleur-de-lis (women prefer to throw a silk scarf around their shoulders). This is often followed by a sort of suicidal despondency in which the patient longs for the glorious days of the monarchy, even though, had he known them, he would have surely lived in the extreme poverty and scorn reserved for commoners. This sickness may remain in a state of benign incubation for years, but once the patient has lost his sense of the ridiculous, he is lost, body and soul.

This was what lay in wait that autumn of 1976. I wasn't just a gardener: I was a gardener at Versailles. My father, who had always had a certain sympathy for the royalist agenda, actually cried out, "We're finally returning home" when he heard I had been hired. Idiot that I was, I was overjoyed to know that, for the first time, he was finally proud of me. What a triumph I felt when the mechanic in Celle-Saint-Cloud asked me if it was true that I worked at Versailles. The pomp and circumstance of state visits to which I often played spectator never ceased to impress me. And what a change with the girls! I still found myself as ugly as ever, and perhaps they did too, but from then on I had an entire array of means to make myself more interesting to women: a job to impress them, a paycheck to reassure them, and a playground fit to fulfill their dreams. What a bonus! Walking a girl down the garden path is a centuries-old strategy for seduction, and now I was the one who had planted the garden. The attention that I had waited for during my entire adolescence was finally coming my way, en masse, thanks to Versailles. I didn't do much in those days to improve the beauty of the grounds—I was barely capable of carrying out the decisions made by my supervisors, but I was the one who could be found in the garden every day, the one the tourists photographed, the one who gave directions to lost visitors and posed with each member of a busload of magnificent Scandanavian women…"*et moi, et moi, et moi,*" just like the Dutronc song I hummed every morning.

✿

I WAS ONLY an apprentice gardener's assistant and there was nothing royal about my daily routine. I got up early. Around seven fifteen I went to the little bistro that used to be next to the Orangerie to drink my coffee. The place was frequented by two charming alcoholic security guards. We all have little signs that help us know whether we're on time in the morning. My variation on the water clock was based on the number of glasses of white wine that had been consumed by my colleagues. When they were on their first *petit blanc,* I would order; by the second, my coffee would be cool enough to drink; and by the third, I knew I had best hurry if I didn't want to be late. At seven thirty I hastily put on my work coat in the glacial chill of the Orangerie, and sometimes even the mittens my mother had given me. By ten I was already feeling sleepy and always volunteered to carry the leaves to the depths of the garden to be able to take a fifteen-minute nap, resting my head on the tractor's steering wheel, which invariably left a telltale mark. The work of a gardener, in those days, was exhausting—more ditch-digger than florist—as a result, it's no surprise that gardening is largely a masculine profession. It was work that required physical strength. We gathered fallen leaves with pitchforks and tossed them up into a wagon, every day from September to March. When a tree was cut down, we chain sawed and loaded the wood ourselves. Today the backhoe does the heavy lifting. The world of gardeners was long a world of men, and not all of the flowers in the greenhouse grew in pots—some of them decorated the pinup calendars that hung from the walls. In another sign of progress, along with the back-hoes, women disappeared from our calendars and entered the profession. But in 1976 we were a community of men. After long days I was exhausted, especially with the added nightlife, to which my coworkers had introduced me at the Cinévog of Saint-Lazare.

The rest of the story went by too fast. In less than five years I had climbed the ladder of manhood. I met a young woman named Cathy and wooed her, telling her about my apartment at the Orangerie. Not long afterwards, she joined me. This was a fatal error—I had hardly left the family nest than I found myself plunged into the embraces and restraints of married life. My apartment might have been at Versailles, but it was far from *being* Versailles. It was a studio—already small for one person and quite clearly insufficient for two. What was more, our family soon grew. Sébastien was born when I was hardly twenty-three, and Justine came five years later. No sooner had I escaped the torments of adolescence than I found myself a father. Looking back, I see how ignorant we were, but I think that, paradoxically, if we acted so irresponsibly, it was out of hunger for responsibil-ity. At the same time, I started to pass professional exams. First I became what is called a *jardinier mosaïste*—I trimmed and remodeled the lacy patterns of boxwood imagined by Le Nôtre. I was happy to be at the head of a team, especially since I knew all of my men so well, but the greatest pleasure came with the possibility of redesigning certain spaces. I was trusted with the north parterre, but after two years, I had had enough of the strict lawns with their eternal begonias and low-cut grass, which I felt were below the standards of the rest of the park. Little by little, I started introducing flowers that had more of a country feeling. A park, to me, ought to be alive, not a mausoleum of flowers ready for embalming. In my stride, one that, happily, wasn't interrupted by military service, I was admitted to the exam to become *sous-chef jardinier*, and as the top-ranked candidate, it was easy to get assigned to Versailles. As strange as it might seem outside of France, the position was that of a public servant, thus allowing me to fulfill my civic duty on the grounds. The state, or rather, the Ministry of Culture, decides whom to hire based on its needs and the number of people who retire. Not long afterwards I became the youngest head gardener in the history of Versailles, a position that didn't take long to stir up a certain degree of envy and jealousy, throwing a few wrenches into the works.

Administrating the park of Versailles is somewhat like being at the head of a company. With its 2,100 acres of terrain and more than a hundred employees, it's a veritable dominion. The grounds require an enormous amount of care and cause no end of worries. Every day I have to make decisions about new projects and delegate work to a large number of personnel from different walks of life: team leaders, gardeners, apprentices, citizens sentenced to community service, and employees hired by our subcontractors. My duty is to ensure that the park remains presentable, respecting the needs of both the tourist and the soul of the place. There is a risk of turning the grounds into an extension of the museum, gardens "under glass" where people can't sit down, picnic, or touch a blade of grass. To the contrary, I try to make the garden a place where people can live, where the visitor can come as much for the history as for some fresh air, jogging, or just a walk. Versailles has always served as a green space for Paris. Once the hunting grounds of Louis XIII, the park is still a place where city dwellers can get back in touch with nature. I'm proudest of having kept the authenticity of Versailles alive. Walking on my thick, bucolic lawns, the visitor doesn't realize the enormous amount of maintenance that their air of neglected beauty requires. The opening of the Trianon's lawns to the public was also one of my great victories. If the day following their visit to Versailles a person still remembers an odor or image of their experience, I've succeeded in my mission.

STILL, MODERN GARDENS have their own seven plagues. For example, we have to fight against all sorts of different insects. I try to give preference as much as possible to natural solutions and avoid pesticides that are harmful to birds. The environment and its protection are at the center of our concerns. The people working in the château have to look after a museum, a place that is long "dead," but those of us in the gardens are responsible for keeping the park alive, for looking after its health and soul. The conservation of trees has become a top priority. A few years ago, cutting down a three-hundred-year-old tree was a regular occurrence. Today, we do everything we can to protect these ancestral monuments. Our oldest specimens are the colossal oak, about 361 years old, which stands near the Grand Trianon, a Japanese pagoda tree that was planted at the end of the reign of Louis XV, and the "Revolutionary" plane tree in the Queen's Hamlet. To these can be added one or two trees that date to the reign of Louis XIV, four or five from the time of Louis XV, and a dozen or so from the days of Louis XVI. Without the intervention of my illustrious predecessors these numbers could probably be multiplied by two, but I'd rather not think about it. There is no use reprimanding people for having been in touch with their time—especially in those days when the priority was modernization, not eliminating waste.

In recent years, we have tried to plant flowers that might seem less impressive but which are probably more authentic. Roses in particular have undergone so many changes that they have often lost their scent. They have become floral postcards, odorless invalids—visually perfect, but with none of the old emotion. To me, a garden without scent is a garden doomed to oblivion. Instead of these insipid varieties, we choose to plant little roses that are almost like wildflowers and which go by the charming name *cuisses de nymphes*. From this point of view, my line of work is radically different from that of my predecessors. Richard, the gardener of Louis XVI, presented the queen with the first cinerarias to be grown at Versailles. Nearly 250 years later, I was proud to show Christine Albanel, the president of the château, a new variety of rose called Petit Trianon, which was selected for the gardens by the Meilland nursery. It was created with love and emits a sweet and delicate perfume. Scented roses are finally back!

Another modern plague, but one that is more touching, are tourist buses. The children stamp down the lawns and, more unexpectedly, the grandmothers steal plants. The buses full of seniors pull up—I love them—and a hoard of retired women in their Sunday best, hair fixed (inevitably blue and enveloped in a cloud of rice powder that I long mistook for dust). They lead the way, chatting loudly, while a few men drag behind, doddering and stricken by the loss of their wives. The merry widow is anything but a myth. These grandmothers are the queens of plundering—they smell the flowers, comment, go into ecstasies, and then give a final glance over their shoulder before savagely ripping up entire plants—that is, when they don't take the pots as well. What is there to say? What could I do when they told me they lived through two wars and that some forty-eight-year-old kid isn't going to tell them what good manners are? I'm quite incapable of making the slightest reproach. It's the same with the little children whom we see triumphantly bringing their mothers bouquets picked out of our gardens.

Of course, there are also what I call the "problems of the day"—a part of the job that I love. There is always something to do, to repair, to save, or to fix up. One day it's a leak, another day a trellis to repair, or a flowerbed to fill in. These are little chores, but the beauty and health of the gardens depend upon them. Then there are all the little daily intrigues—love stories, of course, but also darker affairs, and sometimes theft. This round of activity has nothing to do with my professional obligations, but I know the gardens like the back of my hand and I like a bit of adventure. A lost child? I set off on a rescue mission—there aren't that many places a person can get lost or hide in the park, and after thirty-eight years at Versailles, I know them all. I rarely get it wrong, thanks to experience, no doubt, but most of all to curiosity. I've always got an eye on things. A good gardener is used to analyzing the silent signals that the park sends him. My office has a broad bank of windows, and even I when I shouldn't be, I'm on the lookout. I think it was Choron who gave me the bad habit. All this, in sum, is the life of a gardener at the Château de Versailles in the twenty-first century.

Regrettably, my days are much like those of a CEO. I most enjoy designing flowerbeds, caring for old trees, and orchestrating plantings, but giving orders, administrating, and managing a budget of many hundreds of thousands of euros are the imperatives that impose themselves upon my schedule. Up early in the morning, I always start by going to see the gardeners in the greenhouses—to encourage them, of course, but also to keep myself informed. I think the people in the greenhouses are more aware of our problems than the various outside consultants we hire, who seem only to think about how they can make us pay even more for reports which, more often than not, are pointless. The rest of the morning is given over to reading these reports and various similar chores. The administration of Versailles has become increasingly cumbersome with the passage of time. Beyond the absurd security measures that have been imposed, what was once a minor piece of paperwork now feels more like a novel. Hiring a simple temporary worker now necessitates filling out nearly forty pages of paperwork.

We're also in a perpetual struggle to find funding. Versailles— like all gardens belonging to the French state—is administered by the Ministry of Culture which, apart from a few rare occasions, is more interested in underwriting circus and theater acts. The ministry only gets involved when it comes time to hire a master craftsman. The proof of this can be found in the changes to our official titles that occurred in the late 1980s: the word *art* had to be used! Le Nôtre was just a head gardener, but nobody today would call into question his talent. It seems the garden just isn't chic enough for the world of the arts and culture, although our funding has improved in recent years. Could it be that our ministers have developed green thumbs? For my part, I'm not sure that my line of work is really an artistic discipline. I think it's more of an *art de vivre*—an art of living well and helping people live well. The title changes resulted in a significant proportion of our personnel, starting with me, being obliged to take more official exams in order to have the honor of becoming a *"technicien d'art."* Today there are no more simple gardeners at Versailles.

My afternoons are less routine. I usually leave the office to check up on various projects. There are the big undertakings that give a rhythm to the year. In September I visit the beds and borders to note which plants aren't blooming anymore and which are still producing color. My colleagues and I decide on the layout for the following year. In January we put the final touches on the project and by April, everything is ready to go. In recent years we've gone back to using potted plants, a feature that hadn't been part of the gardens since the time of Louis XVI, apart from the orange trees. This is an idea that I'm particularly proud of, along with that of banning cars from the park. I, of course, didn't sign off on the final decision, but I think that I regularly harassed my superiors about it for a good fifteen years. The park is much cleaner and safer now that it is a pedestrian zone, and the wildlife has also started to come back. Cars caused many problems: roadkill, accidents, exhibitionists, and drug dealers mostly belong to the past now.

In the evening, I make my last round through the gardens in the company of my German shepherd, whose walks I fit in according to the schedule of the day or the day to come. Around ten in the evening, I return to my office to see to my various personal occupations, including my writing, contemplating the view from the large window that overlooks the sleeping park. Living at Versailles causes me to sometimes confuse my job and my life: I didn't have a calling to become a gardener, but it has become my passion.

# STROLLING THROUGH THE PAST
≈≈≈≈≈≈≈≈≈≈≈≈≈≈≈≈≈≈≈≈≈≈≈≈≈≈≈≈≈≈≈≈≈

"IN THIS CHARMING and royal house to which you, the curious and learned people of the world are invited to visit, you will find both the ancient Rome and the Rome of today; you will see all things of beauty and astonishment that the world has ever known." The eighteenth century has retained the label *grand siè-cle*. No doubt the emphasis placed on its greatness was equal to its grandeur, as testify the words of Racine's predecessor as court historian, Louis Moret. This self-confident century didn't shy away from words or excess: Versailles *was* the center of the world.

The majesty of classic style doesn't click with my personality or profession. I'd be too worried about becoming like the fabled frog that wanted to be as big as an ox, only to burst. What do you expect? A gardener could only take sides with La Fontaine, a man of nature and insignificant things. As to the game of deciding whom from the past I would have liked to know, the facetious author of the *Fables* would be my choice from the *grand siècle*, and perhaps Molière, as well. The Versailles I want to share is neither grand nor precious; that Versailles I am willing leave to the historians and curators. The story I want to tell is one of a simple, intimate, and, I think, unknown Versailles—a gardener's Versailles.

In the beginning, the place was far from one of pomp and splendor. It all began, appropriately enough, with a garden, or rather, a forest. The year was 1607 and the six-year-old future Louis XIII went hunting with his father for the first time on lands that were said to be well populated with game. The woodlands and heath abounded in animals of all sorts. Hunting in those days was both an art and a necessity from which the king himself was not exempt. Of course His Majesty didn't have to worry about feeding himself or his family, but being a good hunter was a talent that every accomplished man, or more precisely, every gentleman, was expected to possess—it was nobles who hunted; the rest of the world had to poach. In the early seventeenth century, one called the dogs by sounding the horn, pursued the deer, and flushed game on the forest paths of Versailles. I don't have much respect for hunters, particularly those of today—massacring poor animals at no risk to oneself seems like a cruel pleasure. If in those times hunting was a question of survival, today the adjective "ferocious" seems more appropriately applied to the hunter than to the hunted. Still, the hunter's language is peppered with charming and old-fashioned words that I find touching. They sound so French! *Canepetières*, *francolins*, and *outardes*[1] evoke

---

1. Translator's note: A *canepetière*, or *outarde canepetière*, is a little bustard, a formerly prized game bird, now rare, that was once common throughout Europe. The term *outarde* refers in general to this family of game birds, (the bustards), of which several other varieties were also hunted. *Francolins* are pheasant-like game birds.

animals, of course, but more than that, they speak of a lost world, both rural and medieval, the world in which Versailles was born. In those times Versailles was just a small village among others, with a manor house and a priory, a communal oven for baking bread, a mill for grain, and a hangman's tree for justice. That was all. There was nothing special about the place, apart from its privileged geography: On the roads to Brittany and Normandy, it was the last stop before Paris and its five inns were often full. Moreover, it was already a place where Parisians could enjoy nature, and it was easily accessible, particularly from the Left Bank.

Henri IV was the first to truly discover the area. He came regularly to hunt. Not a king overly worried about conventions, Henri was a free spirit who resisted the constraints of court, constraints that were nothing when compared with the complicated etiquette that weighed upon the court under Louis XIV. He would come to Versailles without his entourage, almost incognito. He had his dinner at the inn—what was the point in building a palace? François I had built châteaux along the length of the Loire and the old Louvre was castle enough for Paris. On more than one occasion I've noted how the monarchy still manages to stir up people's emotions—the bitterness of some, the fervor of others. In a word, the institution is part of a past that the French have trouble letting go of. Still, of all their leaders, Henri IV alone is still unanimously loved in the eyes of the French. The *bon roi Henri* has survived the school books and still manages to rally the French from all walks of life around his unblemished standard. Even de Gaulle and Napoleon aren't remembered as fondly—both great men have their opponents, or at least, like all of us, they receive their share of jealousy. But not Henri IV—it almost seems like his assassin, Ravaillac, was the only one who ever hated him!

Despite his many qualities, Henri was not a king who felt the need to build monuments—he was content with the inn at Versailles. He went there to isolate himself from the world, to hunt, and, I imagine, to womanize. What better place for the "Vert Galant" than this country village? All of his favorite prey could be pursued in one place. His son followed his example and a few years later, the ladies and deer of Versailles were pursued by the young Louis XIII. It should be remembered that the origins of the myth of Versailles have their roots in a forest. Too often I've read or heard that Versailles was a neglected, disadvantageous location. I understand the appeal of the paradox that has the pinnacle emerging from nothing, or even less than nothing—in a certain way it is more interesting to imagine that one of the grandest places in the world was once a desert, but this is a myth. Louis XIV may have been a powerful creative force, but his predecessors were not. Although the area did not have many rivers (making the construction of the Grand Canal such a colossal undertaking, and explaining the recurrent problem of supplying the fountains with water), it was a place close to Paris with abundant game and fertile ground ideal for farming (in those days farmers rarely resorted to artificial irrigation). Hunting and proximity to the capital were, in my eyes, the decisive factors. I like to imagine that wild Versailles, a thousand miles away from what it is today. Sometimes in the depths of the woods, in the spot where we piled the trees after the big storm, I rediscover it—a damp and brushy woodland echoing with strange and sometimes frightening noises, a forest that creaks and cracks, that has a life and soul, or, at least, a presence. I do everything I can to preserve the place and remain in touch with its soul. By keeping out cars we have helped the animals to return. Today it is no longer rare for the attentive visitor to cross paths with a pheasant or worried rabbit. The personnel of the Queen's Hamlet are rightly proud of the presence of a swan (our second swan, in fact), which arrived shortly after the storm and which now seems at home.

If the wild version of Versailles is the one that I like best, it must be admitted that it didn't last long after Henri IV. Soon, the high minds of the day came to feel it was inappropriate for the king to stay at the inn. Louis XIII, who would have given up hunting for nothing in the world, decided to "buy" the area. In those days, the king's whims were quite modest—he bought a clearing in the woods and built a small château whose interior courtyard corresponded with today's Marble Courtyard. Louis XIII was a squirrel among men—he didn't have much of an appetite, he just methodically nibbled away at all of the neighboring parcels of land until he obtained the local rights as a lord over Versailles. Although the king was in a dominant position, he couldn't always obligate the area's nobles to do his bidding. The aristocracy had its say in matters, and in those years before the Fronde,[2] royal power was anything but absolute. Acquiring local rights was particularly important in the feudal system because it meant that the land became part of the *domaine royal*. Matters of justice, for example, were dealt with directly by a royal bailiff and not just a local officer. Furthermore, royal letters enfranchised the area— the local market and the three annual agricultural fairs were free of tax, a rare privilege in the days of Cardinal Richelieu's iron fist (and grasping fingers). The town grew rich and came to number some seven thousand inhabitants. This prosperity was fed in part by expanding the château, which became an elegant building of pink brick with roofs of blue slate, flanked by two wings that ended in little pavilions. A garden was created, and the old manor was demolished to make room for the royal vegetable gardens. A kennel and a tennis court were also built on the estate. A bit farther away, special fences kept the royal stock of deer and stags safe from poachers. A vegetable garden, a ground for hunting—Versailles was still nothing particularly grand—the whole domain was little more than seven acres. It simply served to make the king a bit more comfortable in his favorite escape. Its modern real estate ad might read "a pleasant country house just outside Paris."

---

2. The "Fronde" refers to a period of unrest and civil wars that took place in France during the minority of Louis XIV, in which the old aristocracy attempted to protect their powers against the increasing centralization and dominance of the monarchy.

The tone at Versailles remained unofficial—perhaps this is part of what seduced the king. His main royal dwellings were the Louvre, of course, but also the Château de Vincennes to the east of Paris, and the Château de Saint-Germain-en-Laye to the west, where Louis XIII died in 1643. He enjoyed the privacy and freedom he found at Versailles, in what was his own castle, not one belonging to the "Kings of France." That search for intimacy is, in my eyes, one of the keys to understanding Versailles. Majesty and intimacy are two sides of the same coin and define the character of the place like none other. It all depends on how you look at it—one could come to Versailles to be seen or to hide.

Louis XIV made the château a reflection of his grandeur, ceaselessly expanding and transforming his domain. Under Louis XV the size of the apartments grew smaller again, returning to a more intimate atmosphere. The rooms decorated under Louis XV are graceful little jewels that include the Petit Salon, also known as the Salon des Glaces (not to be confused with the Hall of Mirrors), where sliding mirrored partitions allow for constant changes in the reflections, while also isolating the space from the outside world. The same Louis XV used a system of underground passages, which allowed him, among other things, to appear and disappear according to his desires. His Majesty could choose whether to flee or encourage indiscreet onlookers. A few years later, Marie Antoinette would also seek a means of finding solitude. Of course, the pomp of the Sun King and his emulators has overshadowed other parts of Versailles, which today are all but forgotten, but that is probably why I prefer them. Versailles was also a retreat from the world and a place of leisure and solitude.

Let's return to Louis XIII. Upon his death, Versailles knew its first decline. The village, like the château, was forgotten. His widow, the regent queen, Anne of Austria, and her advisor Cardinal Mazarin, were only happy in Paris, where the seat of power was located in the refined luxury of the Hôtel Tubœuf as well as in the future Palais-Royal. Versailles is a place of exception—it seems to have never known compromise and has always been either all or nothing. For the twenty years between the death of Louis XIII and the beginning of the great construction projects of Louis XIV, nothing disturbed Versailles's peace—not even the plotting of the Fronde, which caused the young Louis XIV to so hate the capital that he always seemed to be trying to avoid. In his wandering, he eventually came upon and chose his spot—the little château where his father had loved to go hunting.

Little is known about the king's personality. No doubt, this capacity for avoiding the low blows of armchair psychology is one of the privileges of great monarchs, or great men in general. Nothing so desecrates a man's memory as saying he was money grubbing, an overeater, or lazy. Even the acid tongue of Saint-Simon couldn't ferret out the king's weaknesses. I've spent hours contemplating Louis XIV's portrait. No matter how long I observe, nothing comes to me. What is there to speak of, beyond the heavy wig and one leg set forward? He represents a riddle. He doesn't even look like a megalomaniac. In any case, I have trouble believing that his nurse, Pierrette Dufour, came and kissed him on the forehead every evening. Only, sometimes, through the stones of Versailles and the statues of the park, do I feel like I understand him just a bit. I imagine that the king, deprived too early of his childhood and his father (he was only four years when his father died, in 1643), sought something paternal in his father's château. Perhaps this was the reason that he came to love it and started wanting to transform it.

Did Louis XIV have something grand in mind when he started modifying the palace? I don't think so. He had just known his first triumph. The story of his anger with his Superintendent of Finances, Fouquet, is well known. Fouquet threw such a glorious celebration in honor of the king at his château Vaux-le-Vicomte, that he paid for his servile arrogance with all of his earthly possessions and prison for life. Louis XIV's extreme reaction is often interpreted as the ire of a wrathful tyrant. I don't subscribe to this—to me it seems almost anachronistic. Far be it from me to deny the despotism of the king, but in 1661, Louis XIV was only twenty-five. I see his punishment as the result of a young man's temper. The irony of the story was that, for the first time, the king intervened directly in a matter of justice and was obeyed. Cardinal Mazarin had just died and the young Louis XIV must have been astonished by the ease with which he was able to shut up his former advisor. This was probably how he got a taste for it…

He found himself not only in possession of all of the extremely wealthy Fouquet's property, but also at the head of the legendary team that had built Vaux-le-Vicomte: Le Nôtre, Le Vau, and Le Brun. The king gave their idle hands the work that needed to be done at Saint-Germain and the Tuileries. Versailles was, in the beginning, a place of escape for the great king—it was there that he went to take refuge in the company of his lover at that time, the charming Louise de la Vallière, surrounded by a small entourage of servants distinguished by their blue and red livery. Versailles was reborn under the star of intimacy, and the modifications made during that period are revealing. While Le Nôtre arranged the gardens, Le Vau set to work constructing the first Orangerie and the Ménagerie. Nothing sumptuous was needed to shelter the king's secret affair, apart from the sweetness of oranges, the milk of his livestock and a veritable Noah's ark! Faced with the bitterness of Paris, the mockery of the nobles, and Colbert's heavy advice, Louis XIV built Versailles as a place for dreaming, materializing the images of his imagination. He who had been raised steeped in the classics and who loved Italian dancing and paintings wanted to give life to the beauty in which he had been educated. This was the reason he favored mythological scenes above all others. The woods and gardens are the theater of ancient legends, and the statues are their actors. As a child, I often transformed my grandfather's garden into a fictional Death Valley, where I triumphed over some five hundred Comanches. The little Louis must have seen himself as Hercules defeating the Lapiths—just a translation of era and upbringing. But the monarch had the will, and above all else, the means to bring the fruits of his imagination into being. Thus, his passion for Louise de la Vallière became the Grotto of Thetis—Apollo, served by nymphs and conquering the versatile and changing Galatea—how better to give expression to the royal fantasy? This is where the megalomania begins, the king morphed from an aesthete into a creative force. His daydreams became material marvels and Versailles was transformed from a peaceful retreat into the imposing palace that we know today.

This was the beginning of a period during which Versailles became a setting where anything was possible. A modest stream flowed through the property, but a royal château needs a drawbridge, and above all else, water and fountains! They were built, on themes corresponding to the spirit of the time: the Enceladus, the Etoile, these grand names express the monumental challenge that represented the construction of Versailles under Louis XIV. The construction of the Grand Canal in under five years marked the height of the king's will to defy and master nature. Over 36,000 laborers worked to create the Grand Canal, the château, and its gardens. Every day men died of diseases, fatal falls, or exhaustion under the king's watchful eye. "I am master of myself as I am of the universe," King Louis could imagine, proudly contemplating his work. Nothing shook this self-importance, not even the poor woman who, it is said, insulted the king the day after her son had died working on his "whorish canal." All she received in return was a sound beating. This about sums up the clemency of Louis XIV, but when compared with the punishment inflicted upon the poor Fouquet, a few blows of the rod seem mild...

It was a monumental undertaking. After the Trianon, the domains of Clagny, Gratigny, and Choisy-aux-Bœufs were bought up. Entire villages, farms, and parishes were destroyed. To complete the project, the forest surrounding the château, the Parc-aux-Cerfs, was swallowed up in 1694. Considered in terms of conquests and buffer zones, the construction of the royal estate was thought out on the same scale as the king's foreign policy. Nothing stopped its expansion. The former inhabitants were forced to leave, chased away both by the royal troops and by the workers and artisans of the construction site. The former were "housed" in a shantytown that had been thrown up at Bel-Air to the north and in the Hôtel de Limoges to the south—the name of which comes from the colonies of workers that came to Versailles to escape the crushing poverty of the Limousin region. Although it's true that the château cost many lives, it provided a livelihood to many more. Mills, lime and plaster kilns multiplied and prospered, to the point that the area grew considerably richer and saw a noticeable increase in its population. Even taking into account the margins of error inherent to such estimates, the population continued to grow into the 1780s. On the eve of the Revolution, the former village counted some 60,000 inhabitants, a number that would not be matched until after the First World War. France as a whole also profited from the construction site. Along with marble from the Pyrenees, tapestries from the Gobelins, and mirrors from the workshops of the Rue du Temple, the nation's best talent was sought out in the creation of Versailles. France had not known a project of such opulence since the time of the medieval cathedrals. From an economic point of view, Versailles was a success from the outset.

Political glory was not long in following. The château soon became the seat of power. The king's secretaries moved into the two wings of ministries, and on the Grand Canal, completed in 1679, there sailed a miniature version of the royal fleet so that the king could witness reenactments of the naval battles in which his men were dying. In the same way that the monarch became mixed up with the idea of the state, Versailles was confused with the kingdom—making it necessary for all of the lifeblood of France to be present, or at least, represented. The king's folly became a royal city, centralizing his power. A charter gave tax advantages to those who built in the town, making it in the utmost interest of the various royal administrators to set up shop nearby. L'Enfant, the architect who would later construct Washington, DC, was given the unheard-of project of erecting an entire town. The royal charter also determined what sorts of buildings could be constructed— low brick pavilions with mansard slate roofs (nothing was to be higher than the château or block the king's view). Historians speak in terms of "absolute monarchy"—but I would go so far as to call it totalitarianism. The king couldn't see into peoples' hearts and souls, but he dominated everything else. At the beginning of his reign, he even had trouble sharing power with divine authority, churches were razed to make way for the construction of the château, which in those times, still had no place for worship. It was only at the very end of his reign that a mere chapel, not even a church, was erected on the grounds. Even here, one senses the influence of the pious Madame de Maintenon, and the infirm and aging king's sense that the end was near.

The king dominated the world because the world was at Versailles. Rare plants and animals were brought from the four corners of the earth. The seventeenth century was a time of gallantry; harmony and beauty guided the hand of Le Nôtre and his assistants, but what better way to subjugate the court than by serving it the affectation it so desired? Domination through aesthetics was perhaps the greatest exploit of the reign of Louis XIV, and the attitude of Madame de Sévigné, the famous epistolarian, on the subject is rather revealing. A proud woman, not in the least submissive, especially since achieving the honorable status of widow, Madame de Sévigné never held back in describing the "prodigious mortality rate of the workers that are carried away by the wagonload every night as though from a hospital"[3] during the construction of the Grand Canal. In her letters she nicknamed Versailles the "meritless favorite" in reference to the king's stubborn pursuit of his projects and the constant delays in its construction. Her proud cousin wrote back, not without a

3. Letter from Madame de Sévigné to Bussy-Rabutin, 12 October 1678.

certain irony, that "it would be a strange misfortune if after having spent thirty million on Versailles it became uninhabitable."[4] The aristocracy still had a say and would continue to ridicule the extravagant king and the fairy-tale castle that many believed doomed to failure.

Less than five years later, Madame de Sévigné wrote to her friend the Comte de Guitaut: "I have just returned from Versailles. I saw the beautiful apartments and fell under their charm. If I had read about them in a novel, I would have been ready to do anything to see them in reality. I saw and touched them and they are an enchanting dream. They have a veritable freedom, not at all what I anticipated. Everything is grand, everything is magnificent, and the music and the dancing are perfection. It was to these two things that I devoted myself, and they helped me enormously in making my way at court, as they are both in their own way a sort of calling of mine. But what pleased me most of all was to have spent four entire hours in the king's company, to be part of his enjoyment and his part of ours; it was enough to content an entire kingdom, one that passionately loves its master. I don't know who had the idea, but God bless them, whoever they are."[5]

The gardens were an excellent means for demonstrating power. Who would dare raise their voice in such a place? Such

---

4. Letter from Bussy-Rabutin to Madame de Sévigné, 14 October 1678.
5. Letter from Madame de Sévigné to Monsieur le Comte de Guitaut, 12 February 1683.

an abundance of beauty imposes silence and respect, especially given that Louis XIV, a great lover of his gardens, was perpetually working to make them even more beautiful. First came Le Nôtre's work, sculpting nature into the dreams of his time and to the glory of his king. What did people dream of in those days? Antiquity, quite visibly: Apollo, the four Nymphs, Galatea and Thetis, all were put into the king's service, as were the light, vegetation, and fireworks, in sum, the four elements, brought together at each of the monarch's appearances and for the festivities organized between 1674 and 1684. The construction projects were perpetual—no sooner had the Grotto of Thetis been completed than it was modified to allow for additional ornaments. Galatea no longer had reason to figure in the garden of a king inspired by a new nymph, Madame de Montespan. Once again, the grounds had to reflect the king's image, down to the slightest vicissitudes. The death of Le Nôtre somewhat slowed the garden's constant expansion, but Jules Hardouin-Mansart took up where Le Nôtre left off, working as an architect and constructing the gardens in the image of the château. The gardens became a sort of green version of stone—urban staircases replaced allées, as testify the Hundred Steps that lead to the Orangerie and the Pièce d'Eau des Suisses. Even the bosquets became civilized, with the Ballroom and the Colonnade evoking rooms in the château. The garden became an ideal city, parallel to the idea city of the palace, one built using the laws and lines of geometry. The king added rare animals and plants that he had brought from all across the globe and that the ingenious La Quintinie did his best to keep alive. Managing to grow figs, Corinth grapes, and orange trees outside of Paris was nothing less than a miracle, and everybody was enchanted with his triumph over nature.

When the court installed itself at Versailles in 1682, it signed its own death warrant—revolt could no longer come from their corner. Flattering songs of praise in honor of the king succeeded one another until his death, with the royal aura seeming to carry along everything in its wake, even talent. The illustrious Racine even gave up his art as a dramatist to become the king's historian; nothing and nobody seemed able to resist the royal authority. In less than a century, a country village had become the center of the world. The king always needed more, and no one force or individual person seemed able to oppose the king's desires. Still, this arrogance and excess had their price, as they always do. Not long after the court's arrival at Versailles, the king had his first attacks of gout and France underwent terrible food shortages. As in all tragedies, the fall came quickly. The Sun King died in the night in 1715, paralyzed and bedridden: the dancer had lost his legs and the kingdom was bankrupt.

For a time, Versailles was cast back into into the shadows, while the first rays of the Enlightenment began to shine in Paris. As soon as the king had died, the Duke of Orléans, (who was to rule until Louis XIV's great grandson, Louis XV came of age), lost no time in returning to the Palais-Royal, whereas the young Louis XV was raised in the Tuileries Palace. Paris's

intellectual life was bubbling with wit. With time, the austere old freethinkers were replaced by adepts in debauchery
(including the Regent, himself a fervent apostle). During this
time, Versailles was gradually abandoned. The Sun King's glit-
tering palace became a sort of Sleeping Beauty. On the eve of
Louis XV's adulthood, the new king, always ready to bestow a
kiss, returned and awakened the palace, restoring the court to
Versailles, where it would stay until October 1789. In the sixty-
seven years between Louis XV's coronation and the Revolution,
Versailles assumed the appearance we know today. Much of the
town was built in the styles Louis XV and Louis XVI. A sign of
the time, the Grand Apartments were abandoned in favor of private spaces where the gallant Louis XV, a worthy heir to Henri
IV, housed his numerous mistresses.

Versailles returned to its intimate past, as seen in the French
Garden's Pavilion and, of course, the Petit Trianon. Marie
Antoinette's whims brought about the final modifications, much
to the domain's benefit. Taken by a need for solitude and nature,
the young Austrian girl brought in her baggage the first breath
of romanticism that was then emerging in Germanic countries,
bestowing Versailles with a Grotto, a Hamlet, and a Temple
dedicated to *amour*. Each of her projects caused a scandal. It
was true that they seemed affronts to the aesthetics of Louis
XIV—the praise of love in response to the Salon de Guerre, the
secretive shadows of the Grotto defying the sparkling reflections
of the Hall of Mirrors, and the rural simplicity of the Hamlet

turning its back on the green citadel of Le Nôtre and Hardouin-Mansart. Louis XVI was no less active: he courageously had the gardens replanted and decorated with the creations of his architect Richard Mique. The château and its grounds were now complete. Versailles underwent no further major changes after 1789.

History continued its work, of course, but I will leave that story to historians. Such ruptures and continuity, the hammer and chisel of time, and the organization of the past require tools unfamiliar to gardeners like myself. Time is very important to us, but I'm afraid that it is a sort of time unrelated to the implacable chronology of history manuals. I've read a considerable number of books on Versailles—from the erudite to the general, from the dense to the laconic, Marxist, structuralist, and royalist studies, works concerning the eccentric, the anecdotic, and the theoretical side of Versailles—rare are the studies of Versailles's history that I haven't at least skimmed. All of them have their moments of beauty, many are amusing, and some even manage to capture a grain of the truth, something of Versailles's character. I have a particular weakness for the now outdated books of Pierre de Nolhac, *La Résurrection de Versailles*, *Le Trianon de Marie-Antoinette*, and *Versailles inconnu*. But none of these has managed to capture the spirit of the place. To a certain degree, this is normal. Historians are not eyewitnesses—they construct knowledge—others transmit experience.

✻

I HAVE LIVED at Versailles for more than thirty years now and feel I have become a witness. My experience and life depend upon these stones, like ivy clambering up a wall. The relationship has become so close that I'm no longer certain whether I have helped to make Versailles or whether Versailles has been responsible for shaping me. The stones communicate knowledge that, although mute, is real and which has nothing to do with the information contained in the work of a historian. This is the sort of knowledge that doesn't come from a book, but which is lived and personal; that is what I'd like to pass down here. I've read a great deal, but more importantly, I've lived, I've patiently watched and listened, and I've loved a place that has given me much—with a love that has made me curious to know more. I've always been interested in the origins of things—perhaps because I've grown distant from my own roots. From this mix of information, my own history of Versailles took shape—a history composed of knowledge that comes as much from my mind as from what I've lived.

The wild escapades accredited to Marie Antoinette are not the work of contemporary historians but pamphlets against the queen written during the Revolution. The poor Marie Antoinette was accused of every vice, or at least, of scandalous encounters she was said to have had in the garden's cover. Anybody who knows the gardens knows that one is never out of sight. The bosquets are ideal for hiding, but they are also ideal for spying; the queen was surely the object of more than one indiscreet onlooker. It seems impossible to me that the garden could have served as the setting for such games of debauchery. To confirm this, one needs only to spend a day in the company of the guards who spend much of their time chasing down exhibitionists and voyeurs. Another space seems better suited to propping up revolutionary rumors: prudishly referred to as the *"salon de spiritisme,"* the room is unfortunately not open to visitors. Situated between the music room and the bedroom, the salon looks out onto the garden through French windows that flood the space with light and allow for everything that is happening in the garden to be seen while simultaneously being seen oneself. No other space stages the royal presence in quite the same way. If the queen wanted to invoke the spirits, two sliding panels could block the windows to plunge the room into darkness. The queen, once quite visible, became invisible. One knew she was present, but did not wish to be seen. It is not entirely clear what the space was used for. The architect supposedly built the room for the royals to "distance themselves from constraint," but it is also said that the queen held séances to communicate with the dead. While there were certainly candles in the room, there are also mirrors on all four of the sliding walls. I have trouble believing they were used for the viewing of glowing bodies, spiritual or otherwise...

With experience, one develops a sort of living memory. The intertwining of the garden and my life is so complete that I sometimes feel like the paintings by Arcimboldo, portraits of men made entirely of fruits and vegetables, the plants that I've spent my life growing—the gardener's ultimate destiny. But the garden has made out better. The information I've accumulated has allowed me to piece together more than one of its puzzles. A few years ago, I read that lotuses once grew in the Pépinière, but no matter how many archives I consulted, no plan or map showed the trace of the sort of basin that they would have needed. The whole story might have ended there had the storm not destroyed part of the Pépinière, and called for some construction work. As my men dug, they came upon an old iron pipe—the stones were gone, but we had rediscovered the old basin!

There is nothing essential about my research, but it has allowed for a better knowledge of the gardens and their plants. In one case, it allowed for the preservation of a particularly old hawthorn. The aged tree had grown so large that it was starting to threaten its neighbors, so I decided to have it removed. Still, the color of its wood and an engraving that I had seen caused me to doubt my conclusions. The engraving, which showed the same part of the garden, clearly featured a hawthorn in the fore-ground. The tree was already of considerable size—and this was in the eighteenth century. Of course, it wasn't unusual to plant the same variety of plant in the same spot, especially something so ordinary as a hawthorn, but to quiet my conscience I ordered the National Forestry Office to make a study of the trees in the sector. The hawthorn turned out to be 250 years old: it had known Louis XV, and I had saved it from getting the chain saw.

Everything is interesting if you know how to observe and listen. In my quest for information, I don't underestimate demonstrations by curators, tales told by veteran employees, or anecdotes from the ticket counters and gardeners. One of the supervisors at the Petit Trianon, Marcel Berton, was a veritable gold mine of information. He had worked at Versailles for more than forty years. One day, in the middle of the 1980s, shortly before his retirement, we were chatting at the foot of Marie Antoinette's oak, a venerable patriarch planted at the entry to the Trianon. He patted the massive root at his foot and began the story about how the tree was already old when he arrived at Versailles and that it hardly seemed any older forty years later as he was preparing to leave. Time is harder on the rest of us. As the French song goes, "a gardener has never died in the memory of a rose," but this does not hold true for a tree, which typically watches three or four generations come and go. I comforted my supervisor with a line of poetry about the anonymous, timeless beauty of our trade. Reassured to see he had been understood, he told me that he had watched over the oak since 1960 and that he had heard from the old gardeners in his day that it had once been surrounded by a low wall. He didn't know where the story had come from, and it was unverifiable without digging up the park's crown jewel. A few years later, the tree fell victim to drought and died. Remembering the words of Marcel Berton, I asked the gardeners to take care removing it. Scattered among the roots we discovered the remains of old paving stones—the wall had indeed existed—case closed. Marcel Berton, in the face of all the books on the garden and its history, had been correct.

He never wrote a book himself, but he allowed for a discovery to be made, and thanks to him, a little piece of history had been uncovered.

Nothing makes me happier than finding something that isn't found in any book. If good old Berton was a wonderful guide, he wasn't alone: I owe as much to the many curators that have deigned to try to teach me something. If there is a place in Versailles for which I feel an unflagging love, it would be Marie Antoinette's theater. Small and welcoming, it was used for the queen's private performances. She not only had artists come to entertain her, but she herself was also known to take the stage— she had an actress's soul and loved to sing. What a strange life, that princess who dreamed of becoming a shepherdess! It is said that she was talented, although I would be more inclined to believe she had good teachers and a great many flatterers. But it is certain that she had taste, because the theater is adorable— a real little doll's house with seating for sixty and a large stage, backdrops imitating a leafy garden, and hanging above it all, the majestic golden letters "M. A.," a reminder to visitors of the former owner of this pretty plaything.

Although it is unfortunately closed to the public, the theater was recently restored. Concerned about the future of the miniature theater, I often stopped in to check on the work. The head architect told me about the building's history. Since its construction, little had been changed, apart from the famous "M. A." above the stage, pulled down by the revolutionaries who were disappointed to find nothing of value in what they had thought to be one of the monarchy's treasuries. This made me all the more perplexed to see the shining letters that I had known for years still in place above the stage. When I voiced my confusion, he reminded me that the only modifications since the eighteenth century had been made under Louis-Philippe, a great theater lover who offered the stage to his wife, Marie-Amélie.

One day, a storm uprooted a tree, leading my colleagues and me to discover an underground passage that ran to the back of the Trianon. I compared the various maps and engravings I own as well as those conserved in the château archives to which I have access. I was finally able to identify and date the mysterious passage, which had slumbered unnoticed for decades, undoubtedly one of the many tricks for crossing the gardens without being seen. During the Revolution, or perhaps even before, the secret had been forgotten. On the day we rediscovered it, I was one of the few people who knew about that secret tunnel in the depths of the gardens.

The visual knowledge of the park acquired over almost forty years is an asset in my work. I know exactly when the rhododendrons of each allée go into bloom, what part of the park might need repairs, and in which areas the public tends to behave or misbehave. My policy is essentially to leave the gardens to themselves. For a long time, the gardens' lawns and flowerbeds were all carefully manicured. It's only recently that we've tried to return the gardens to their former appearance. Paintings have proved to be particularly precious sources of information. Who would have thought that I would one day so carefully scrutinize the countless paintings that hang in the château! The Galerie des Cotelle in the Grand Trianon is a treasure trove of historical details. The kings loved the gardens so much that they ordered paintings of them to decorate their interiors. The works of Jean Cotelle are, in my eyes, more decorative than artistic, but they provide a great deal of information about gardening in his time. The painter used all of his talent in the in mythological scenes where the bosquets of Versailles serve as backgrounds. If one looks past Venus and the various nymphs, his work is a quasi-photographic view of the park as it appeared in the past. I have even been able to determine what tools where used. I don't much care whether the shepherd portrayed is Celadon or Tityre, the essential thing is that he is holding a wooden rake, and not one of iron—metal tools were still rare then. The yews in the foreground are trimmed into globes and not cones as we shape them today. The orange trees were still being grown in pots. A number of parterres are painted in the background, all planted in the same manner. Four colors dominate—blue, red, pink, and a touch of white. Armed with this information I turned to the archives to see what plants were ordered—and noted that they confirm Cotelle's portrayal. Similarly, his *Montagne d'eau* shows us the animals that could be found in the garden: no horses or carriages, but a great number of dogs. The vegetation is a deep green, showing that the trees were tall, dense, and therefore relatively old. By piecing together bits of information, a bit like a police investigation, we have been able not only to sketch out a history of the garden but to return the garden closer to its former self. Of course, we don't seek to make an exact copy of what Jean Cotelle saw, but rather to respect the aesthetics reflected in his work. The Trianon's parterres are changed yearly, but they always respect the four-color scheme.

Hearsay, discussion, observation, and reading are the sources for my living history of Versailles. The old regulars often come and tell me about what the gardens were like in their childhood, whereas still lifes allow me to figure out the dates that different flowers came into bloom as well as the painter's habits. Peonies and nasturtiums in the same painting are a sign that the painter probably took several weeks to finish his work and that the bouquet as pictured never actually existed, because the last peonies flower about five weeks before the nasturtiums begin to bloom.

Versailles has been the stage for great events that have shaped France, but also a thousand and one smaller adventures that have contributed no less to the identity of the place. When a superstitious gardener plants a tree, he buries a bottle containing a message—a way of signing his work. Although I rarely follow this old custom, I like finding the messages. There is rarely much that is original in the bottles—a date, a name, sometimes a dedication—but the very spareness of the information they contain is also what makes them so moving. History hasn't bothered with these witnesses, but they participated no less in the château's life.

If books sometimes are able to reveal truths, the quiet sounds, stones, and groves of the garden contain their truths as well.

I've tried to read everything that has been written and said about the château. I'm not vain enough to claim to be a specialist, but the books or articles that aren't sprinkled with errors, even minor, are rare, and they sadden me as much as they annoy me. The worst are the accounts that contribute to fabricating a glossy magazine version of Versailles. I've seen my fair share of tour groups filing through the Petit Trianon, and I feel for them—weathering such a marathon of more or less factual information.

"Across from you, the Petit Trianon, built in 1768 for Madame de Pompadour, Louis XV immediately adopted it as his favorite residence. To the left, the *Sophora japonica* planted around 1772." Visitors are informed, but what do they feel? I can't find the warmth of Versailles in such blandness, and I don't think tourists come here in search of information at all. The bus-loads of Japanese tourists and honest grandmothers don't visit the Queen's Bedroom to learn about the particular type of canopy bed she slept in or the sort of wood it is made from; they come to relive a moment in the queen's life.

The guides might explain why the beds are so short—not only because people were smaller, but because they slept sitting up. Lying down in those days was associated with death. Or one might tell them about royal births, once public events. This sort of information tells us more about the queen's status. But visitors don't have the right to relive Versailles. They view from a distance (but don't touch), contemplating a series of lifeless pieces of furniture (now useless), and hearing about a series of events emptied of any concrete significance. In an attempt to preserve the past, it has been slowly killed. Similarly, the statues of the Grand Trianon were brought inside—they were too precious to leave to the elements.

The weary guide reels off his script in a gloomy air that tells his charges he, too, is bored. In the face of such a model, yawns and stretching are inevitable. Then there is the guide who prefers to dominate his group, commanding them like an army in battle. His goal is clearly to reach the end of the gallery as quickly as possible, and the visit takes on the air of a forced march. Finally, there is the overeager type, who regales his group with insignificant details. "It is the twelfth of October, 1775. The solid bronze clock offered by Louis XV to Madame du Barry indicates three o'clock. The young queen of France is only twenty years old, but she is already a beautiful woman. She has come to picnic and enjoy the celebrated *vin de Savoie*. This wine was imported to Versailles for the first time in…"

The group is already thinking about something else. Perhaps these guided tours are only what Baudelaire described as "that sublime function of the cradle," but whatever they aim for, I detest their errors, which often concern the Trianon's parterres, repeated daily in a variety of languages. Until about ten years ago, the fashion was to fill the beds densely, planting flowers every eight inches—this is the source of the legendary "forty thousand plants of the Trianon." But today we use larger, taller varieties, which are planted farther apart. The Trianon only has ten thousand plants, but the guides still haven't changed their scripts. Luckily, Versailles doesn't need to worry about details to remain worthy of admiration!

Some guides don't even have the modesty to respect the history of the Sun King's life. I don't have much sympathy for the illustrious Louis; in fact, I have trouble feeling much of anything for such an impenetrable character. Still, it must be recognized that he had a real passion for his gardens, loving them with an unflinching, unmatchable devotion. In any case, he was far more faithful to the gardens than he was to any of his numerous mistresses. Apart from administrative documents, the king didn't leave much behind in the way of texts. Louis XIV wanted to leave his mark in the stones of Versailles, not in the pages of a book. Still, one of the rare documents he wrote himself concerns the gardens. At the end of his life, suffering from gout and no longer able to walk, he set down the *Manière de montrer les jardins de Versailles* or *How to Show the Gardens of Versailles*, a manuscript that exists in six versions. I have a copy of a facsimile. The fourth version is particularly touching, as it is an autograph copy. It is humanizing to see the marble king's handwriting and I find it amusing to note the royal spelling errors—which were numerous in those days before standardization. The *"Sfinx"* and the *"lésar et l'île royalle"* are among my favorites. I almost feel a twinge of tenderness toward the king who couldn't spell, particularly given my own hesitations when faced with writing the word "*satyre*." The purpose of his work wasn't literary, but instead to control visits to the garden in his absence. The first version was written on the occasion of a visit from the Queen of England, Marie-Béatrice d'Este. In a clipped and martial style, the king indicates his itinerary point by point, leaving nothing to chance, down to the day and hour of the visit, July 19 at six o'clock in the evening. This is the moment of the day when shadows begin to lengthen, adding supplementary depth to the garden's geometry. Even the pauses in the itinerary are decreed by the king. "Upon leaving the château from the vestibule of the Marble Courtyard, proceed to the terrace. Here one must pause at the top of the stairs to take in the arrangement of the flowerbeds, the lakes and the fountains."

The poor queen was no freer in her movement than in what she was to look at. "Then proceed directly to the top of the Latone and pause to take in the Latone, the lizards, the ramps, the statues and the royal allée, Apollo and the canal. Then turn to see the parterre and the château."

What happened if the queen didn't like statues and preferred to direct her royal eyes upon the topiaries of the parterre? Those were frigid, pleasureless times when even a simple walk was weighed down with protocol and etiquette, both indoors and out.

Still, one has to admit that the king's tours are remarkably effective and offer a complete and harmonious introduction to the garden's features. A military strategist, he had a keen sense of sortie, and as a theater lover, a masterful understanding of staging. The different versions of *Manière de montrer les jardins de Versailles* are due, in large part, to modifications to the gardens. They served to integrate new features to the Colonnade such as *The Rape of Persephone* or the changed positioning of the statues in the Grotto of Thetis. Other changes are linked to the king's illness. The Girandole and the Ballroom would later precede the visit to the Orangerie so that the aging monarch could use the horseshoe-shaped ramps that descend from the Latona fountain and avoid the Orangerie's Hundred Steps. How sad it is to imagine the old king being carted about in luxurious wheelchairs!

If I had to take Louis's place and lay out the itinerary for an ideal tour of the gardens, I would start with neither the Girandole nor the Marble Courtyard. It would be early in the morning, before the gardens are opened to the public, when they are still empty and covered in dew. It would be a bit cool—perhaps it even rained during the previous night—but it would be a beautiful day. It is April, and my only requirement is that my guest enjoys walking. The parterres would smell of freshly cut grass, and we would enter through the side gate so that no modern constructions would mar our view. Coming through the gate, we would see the grounds in the same way that Louis XIV or Louis XV had once seen them. We would walk up to the château, but not by the central Grande Allée. First we would wander through the various bosquets—I would show my guest the places where parties were given, the dark allées where people once schemed in the shadows, the Queen's Grove, where much of the Affair of the Diamond Necklace unfolded, and the lovers' hideaways, where Louis XIV teased his mistresses. We wouldn't spend much time in the château. Its long corridors were made for people to run into each other, plot, gossip, and be seen. Since the disappearance of the court they don't serve much of a purpose, and I would spare my companion the exhausting indoor marathon from which one most often emerges with a stiff neck.

The fate of the average tourist at Versailles is hardly enviable. No sooner have they arrived, by bus or suburban train— forms of mass transport entirely worthy of their French adjective "*commun,*" for there is nothing royal about them—then the poor souls are sent to stand in line and listen to crying babies and sighs of exhaustion. There are also the traditional line jumpers and, more recently, the steely surveillance of security agents in search of abandoned luggage and potential terrorists. Once they overcome this initial ordeal, they are rewarded with a tour of a château so crushed full of people that only the ceilings are visible (hence the stiff neck). Of course, it is forbidden to touch anything, let alone to sit down or take one's time, because another tour group is right on their heels. For the curators who think only of protecting the château and its contents, any outside presence spoils and disturbs their work. This is the reason that tourists are, above all else, a nuisance. Visitors are merely tolerated, and the most that can be said is that nothing is done to encourage them to return. In this sanctuary of the past they have only been shown that they are unwelcome. This is generally the moment when, crazed and breathless, the tourist finally gets a bit of rest in the gardens. Free and open, one can sit, touch the flowers, and even have a picnic. I regret that a system hasn't been put in place to charm visitors and encourage them to return.

In the château, I would only take my visitor to the rooms that, to me, symbolize the two great "stars" of Versailles: Louis XIV and Marie Antoinette. There is no doubt that both have become myths in their own right—they are the figures who, for the large part, retain Versailles's power to fascinate. We would pass through the Salon de Paix and the Salon de Guerre to the Hall of Mirrors, all of which date from the time of Louis XIV. Then we would go to the Queen's Bedroom. After a quick look at the spectacular decor, I would open the hidden door that leads to the private apartments where the rulers actually lived, laughed, worried, or relaxed. The Grand Apartments were reserved for protocol, for the staging of daily life, when the king or queen appeared to receive courtiers, but their private lives unfolded on the other side of doors that the monarchs were careful to close behind them. The most popular exhibition in all my time at Versailles was called "The Royal Tables." Knowing about Louis XIV's political views is instructive enough, but it's far more agreeable to learn that he liked to eat a pear for dessert. This is what I like to call "rifling through history's drawers" and I think it's the sort of behavior we ought to be more indulgent towards—it's so human!

Still, this sort of prying can't go on forever. My ideal visitor and I would step out into the gardens to admire the view of the Grand Canal, the broad lawn, and the parterres before turning right and heading to the Trianon. I would probably tell them about Le Nôtre's tricks for making the perspective seem broader and more open than it really is. If my visitor is one of those marauding old ladies whom I adore, I'd promise a detailed description of the flowers in the northern parterre and my techniques for making sure they get off to a good start after planting, and since I'm bound to be in an excellent mood on this ideal tour, I would probably even offer her a cutting or two. We would only pass through the Grand Trianon to better spend our time lingering in the sumptuous salons of the Petit Trianon, admiring the furniture and delicate charm of these rooms. We would finish with the most enjoyable part of the grounds, in my eyes: Marie Antoinette's country garden. If one sought the origin of the idea of a "secret garden," one would find it here: the spot positively breathes calm and privacy. This is one of the rare places in Versailles where one feels alone, protected and enveloped by the surrounding nature that presses in like a Chinese garden, accentuating the greenery's depth. The queen escaped the oppressive protocol of the court in this garden for which she created her own set of rules. Her etiquette was flexible, relaxed, cordial, and ultimately, fed the fantasies of the republican opposition and the slanderous pamphlets published in the Low Countries. I know of no greater libel than Talleyrand's accounts of this sweet way of life at the end of the ancien régime. But let's not dwell on such Puritanism and instead step back into the exquisite gardens of the Trianon...Frogs are croaking, hidden beneath the long branches of the weeping willow and in the tall reeds. We might linger as we walk past the Grotto or the Temple of Love, passing through the Belvedere and the French Pavilion. Perhaps my guest and I would reveal secrets to one another in the places meant for relaxation and seduction. If my visitor was a woman, it would be in the Queen's Hamlet that I would kiss her, in homage to Marie Antoinette Josèphe-Jeanne de Habsbourg-Lorraine, the Queen of France, Navarre, and Versailles.

# GARDEN STORIES,
# GARDEN HISTORIES
≈≈≈≈≈≈≈≈≈≈≈≈≈≈≈≈≈≈≈≈

P ARALLEL WITH THE history of France are smaller stories from Versailles, which may not have affected History with a
capital H, but remain in our memory because they are so touching and human. Each, in its way, reveals something about the
gardens, and I'd like to tell a few of them here.

The first is a tribute to the man who will forever be the master of Versailles, the great Louis XIV. The setting is the northern
parterre, just in front of the château, where the statues seem to
emerge from the bosquets like the dancing girls that jump out of
cakes in old gangster movies. One of them, standing in a distant
corner, is an allegory of Eloquence. At second glance, Eloquence
turns out to be Louis XIV himself. Although young, he is still
recognizable by the pinched expression that I find a bit ridiculous. He is in his favorite pose, one foot in front of the other,
back straight, his head turned to the side. The statue makes it
clear that the king did not like to be seen in profile. Allegory and
mythology were in fashion in those times, and it was considered
normal to associate Greek heroes with the great names of the
day, turning them into veritable idols. I think it must have been
a sort of game to stroll along the allées of the gardens and guess

who had been transformed into Cleopatra or Hercules—a sort of "who's who" or masked ball in stone. After all, those were also times when riddles and romans à clef were all the rage. In the king's vicinity stand other allegories, including the willowy silhouette of the huntress Diana just across the way. The two statues seem to be looking at one another—a rather unusual positioning. What could Eloquence and the wild goddess be communicating through their frozen gazes? Who is the beautiful huntress?

She was none other than one of the king's favorite mistresses. The statues were an amusing way to make their relationship both public and eternal. This we know—but the huntress's identity remains a mystery. In classical mythology, those who gazed upon Diana suffered the consequences: Acteon died for it, devoured by Diana's hounds, and Endymion was plunged into eternal sleep. Louis XIV as Eloquence was lucky and got out of the situation with little more than a scandal. At Versailles, where seeing and being seen were so important, a glance from the king, even in stone, was not insignificant. Louis intended to dominate others through his own image, and in this sense he was very modern. He spoke little and wrote even less, but he put himself on display. His entire life and person were choreographed. Activities as ordinary as getting up and going to bed were carefully staged, and even set to music, like the ballets he so loved. The gardens were, in this sense, an excellent means of expressing his power.

The Sun King's wife, Queen Maria Theresa of Spain, was never given much attention. She had no choice but to rest in the shadows, and must have been made of solid stuff, seeing how she put up with his countless mistresses. Her passivity would have been remarkable even were the king discreet, but Louis XIV had little time for clandestine love affairs and always set up his favorites (and after them, their illegitimate children) in close proximity and with considerable ado. In honor of Madame de Montespan, for example, the king had Jules Hardouin-Mansart build the Château de Clagny, which he later willed to her and her children. Maria Theresa remained placid. She was so docile and retiring that upon her death in 1683, Louis XIV is said to have remarked, "This is the only grief she has ever caused."

Still, it is said that the queen was so irate following the affair of the statues that she had yews planted between them so that their gazes would no longer meet. Today the trees are gone and Louis XIV eloquently leers at the beautiful Diana once again. I like this story because it softens the image of the distant Louis and gives him the human quality of humor, which I find so important. I can imagine him sternly ordering the statues, delighting at his ruse on the inside. Was he able to keep the secret, or did he confide in the reliable Dagneau, whom he regularly asked to write his love letters? Whatever the case, the statues' unveiling must have been a choice moment, with the king delighting at the surprise of those who understood, the frustration of those who did not, and the anxiety of those who were not sure. Perhaps he watched his public declaration of infidelity from afar, spying upon his gossiping courtiers from the palace windows. Perhaps, grown old and pious, he still gave a mischievous glance at the Diana of his youth while strolling through the gardens in the company of Madame de Maintenon. What did he feel for the women he had seduced? He gave them grand houses; the more he was charmed, the grander the house. Madame de Montespan inherited an entire part of Versailles, Madame de Maintenon received Saint-Cyr, and the young Duchess of Fontanges would have gotten Marly if she hadn't died so young. Beyond these gifts, one can only speculate. In the end, it is in stone that I find a bit of the king's flesh and feel that I begin to understand a character whose very life has always seemed carved from marble. La Bruyère wrote, "The court is a marble edifice, by which I mean to say, composed of men who are hard, but polished."[6] Polished, majestic, and intimidating though he was, Louis XIV was also human.

His great-grandson, Louis XV, inherited this quality. One only has to look at his portraits to feel as though one knows him. With his roguish, sensual, and gentle figure, he seems at once approachable, even kind...to my eyes at least. After an initial period of adoration, he soon became one of France's most hated kings. Assassins have struck out at kings across the ages and Louis XV's was named Damien. He tried to stab the king as he was walking through the gardens, missing his mark but managing to give the king a nervous breakdown. It was less than glorious for a king to burst into tears in public. The royal humiliation, more than the failed assassination

---

6. La Bruyère, *Les Caractères*, "On the Court."

attempt, condemned the poor Damien to forty-five hours of torture finished by pouring molten lead into his wounds. Louis XV personally attended the punishment and asked it to be drawn out several times—it seems he got his nerves back in the end.

I can imagine what sort of man he must have been—nonchalant, a big eater, haughty, and, of course, a notorious womanizer. It is said that a cardinal often reproached the king for his escapades by scolding him, weary but accusing, "Your Majesty, the Queen, the Queen!" The king ultimately heeded the cardinal's reproaches—after all, it is never a good idea to let rumors run wild, even when one is king. I also suspect that he was afraid, for although it was the century of Enlightenment, the fear of hell was a reality from which a king of divine law could not expect to escape.

The debauched king invited the cardinal to take his meals at the Trianon—an honor that could not be refused—and the cardinal was probably already imagining himself the next Mazarin... The man of the church found himself sitting at a table alone. His confusion only grew when at each meal he was served turkey, and always prepared in the same manner.

One evening Louis XV finally came to see him, and the cardinal exclaimed, "Your Majesty, I don't understand: turkey, always turkey, nothing but turkey!"

To which the king replied, "The queen, always the queen, and nothing but the queen!"

❁

LOUIS XV TRANSFORMED the Parc aux Cerfs into a sort of open-air bachelor pad. It is said that mothers came to offer him their daughters. It was undoubtedly an honor to be chosen by the king, and the young Louis had the reputation of being quite personable. Madame de Pompadour had already had her share of his attention and took great care in educating the king's new conquests. The girls were chaperoned and put up in a little house on the Rue Saint-Médéric, not far from the château. When they became mothers, they were given a dowry and married off. Louis XV even had his own personal "taster"—charging one of his valets with testing the young women and keeping a careful record of their particular characteristics—an agreeable enough occupation, but rather risky in those days of syphilis. If, after fifteen days the valet remained free of chancres and pustules, the good king would honor the young lady with a visit. The technique remained foolproof to the end—to the end of the king, that is: he died of smallpox. In a matter of years, his reign had turned the park into a bordello and the local mothers into pimps.

I'm all the more offended by these crimes because Louis also had a real passion for botany. Like that of his illustrious ancestor, Louis XV's love of gardens was as sincere as it was informed. He took great pleasure in, among other things, pushing his wheelbarrow through the gardens—and it is to him that we owe the breezy and bucolic *style champêtre*. He was such a nature lover that he even had a grave dug for one of his deer. Beginning in 1749, he had the area northwest of the Trianon transformed into gardens and in 1768 he built the irresistible Petit Trianon, which he had intended to offer to the equally irresistible Madame d'Etiolles, the Marquise de Pompadour. After building a new menagerie, he added the delightful French Garden, placing a little pavilion (known as the French Pavilion) in its center. I love this place— everything is charming, springlike, and celestial, right down the name of its architect, Gabriel. To the east, Louis XV asked the botanist Bernard de Jussieu to create a botanical school. Here, the gardener Claude Richard grew strawberries and geraniums and even managed to plant the first coffee plants in France. You can understand why the woman to whom we owe the Trianon and the French Garden deserves my profound admiration and recognition! Cultivated and refined, Madame de Pompadour encouraged the king's passion for nature.

The French Pavilion is a marvelous translation of this passion. Constructed at ground level and connected to the exterior through multiple French windows, it allowed the king to view his gardens, no matter the weather. The decor is harmonious—not a single garland, wainscot, or brocade departs from the *champêtre* theme. In the place of the chubby-cheeked cherubs and muscular Moors of Versailles are golden bees, floral garlands, and sheaves of wheat. The ceilings replace the usual allegories of victory (which was, admittedly, far less frequent under Louis XV) with the four seasons.

The French Pavilion possesses another feature I particularly love. It served as the setting for numerous dinner parties

organized for the king by Madame de Pompadour, and later by
her truculent replacement, Madame du Barry. Amid decor evoking the bounty of nature, with the deities Ceres and Flora on the
threshold of every door, there was no question of running short
on food—especially since one needed all the energy one could
get for the lengthy card games organized by Madame du Barry.

The eternal buffets that ornamented the pavilion with abundance seemed to be replenished by magic. Louis XV had a delicate nature—watching servants clear tables, scrape plates, and
collect glasses was not to his taste and he sought to spare others
such disagreeable sights. He was also particularly sensitive to the
need for privacy and had built the Trianon to isolate himself from
the court, preferring the company of a few familiar friends. The
court, of course, took offense—one has to consider that the king's
opposition included all of the nobles who had not been invited to
the sumptuous parties organized by the king or one of his favorites. So as not to be bothered with the incessant flow of servants
required for running such soirées, the monarch came up with a
system of pulleys, which allowed the tables to descend through
trapdoors in the floor. Underground, valets and servants hurried about their business, while in the Trianon, the king's guests
enjoyed the best food and the finest wines. The underground
passages beneath the gardens were also used by the king to disappear when he felt like it. A midnight meeting with a lover in
the park? A boring conversation? A plot against his power? The
king would claim to be thirsty, duck into a tunnel, and be free.

He could return to the party when he felt like it—but in every-body's eyes he had at least made an appearance. Even those who hadn't been invited could watch from a distance, through the Pavilion's many windows. Once again, the gardens of Versailles play with seeing and being seen. With his statue of Diana, Louis XIV revealed a secret affair of the sort his great-grandson pre-ferred to hide. Two men, two different attitudes: the perfection-ist and the manipulator.

Perhaps even more than Louis XV, Marie Antoinette was particularly attached to the gardens of Versailles, especially to the grotto she had constructed by the architect Mique in the Anglo-Chinese garden of the Trianon. For a moment, I'd like to leave reality and propose a fictional walk through these gardens, so propitious to daydreaming…

It is 1779, and I am "well-born" (in my daydreams, I'm rarely poor…). Noble, powdered, and perfumed, with a wig and a lace handkerchief, I hold a title that gives me the right to enter the gardens. (In those times, access to the château and gardens was limited to the aristocracy, recognizable by their hat and sword. It is said that swords were rented outside of the park to allow commoners to enter.) I have been wooing the Marquise de M— for six months (courtship was much longer in those days). For a long time I just observed her from afar during her morning walks before eventually daring to lift my hat to her. I imagine that dur-ing some game of cards she must have asked her friends about my identity, and my political and financial standing. My profile must have been acceptable because, even though she doesn't respond to my greetings, she hasn't changed the itinerary of her morning walks, and the beauty marks and rouge on her delicate cheeks have become more visible. I decide to send her a few sonnets I've written, inspired by her radiant beauty. They haven't been sent back! One evening at dinner, I am even introduced to my delightful Marquise who good-naturedly listens to the compliments I pay her. We discover that we share a passion for the natural sciences, and I offer to show her the charming gardens of the queen, where it is said that one often crosses paths with Monsieur de Jussieu.

Finally we are alone together—another marvelous quality of these gardens was Marie Antoinette's decree that a lady need not be accompanied by her entourage to meander through them. Weary of court protocol, she proclaimed the following rules for her garden, a sort of watered-down version of royal etiquette: no need to bow or to cede the way to the royal family (even though it would probably be more tactful to do so), no need to interrupt one's game of blindman's buff, no need to come with one's servants. I show my beloved the field where the old gardener Richard has planted trees from America and managed to adapt them to the local climate. (America! What a marvelous country! France is in the midst of helping the colonies liberate themselves from English domination.) At the end of the eighteenth century, aristocratic women were cultured and loved the botanical sciences. To conquer my Marquise, it would have been advisable to praise her intelligence before her beauty. I tell her about the wonderful garden we are about to see, planted with lilac, mock orange, and rare trees. Beyond their scientific interest, these specimens have magnificent, delicately scented blossoms. Out of her love of simplicity, the queen wanted everything to seem natural: the grass is not cut, but grazed by sheep.

Our walk leads us to the Orangerie. Here the queen likes to be heard singing, and sometimes acting in comedies. She even had a theater built where she is planning to play in a work by Beaumarchais. My Marquise suddenly becomes serious and assures me that the queen is far too good to give her royal person to acting! The stories about her libertarian leanings are odious slander. The queen loves the arts as she loves her people—that is all. Did she not have the courage, when she was the young Dauphine, to attend the spectacles given at the Royal Opera, weathering the gibes of that dreadful du Barry, whose noble name is due only to a bad joke and bad morals? How could a nobody like du Barry allow herself to refer to the queen as a "redhead"? Didn't the queen open the gardens to commoners once a week? Hadn't she given patronage to artists, even women like Madame Vigée Le Brun, who has just completed a most poignant portrait of her, the queen in all of her beauty, with no jewel other than a simple rose?

The Marquise's praise for the queen is boundless—the queen sings, dances, she even knows how to cook. She glances skyward as she evokes the heavenly carp *"façon Marie Antoinette,"* which she had the immense honor of tasting, prepared by the queen's own hands. I remain silent, thinking of the other stories I've heard about the "Austrian": a woman who would give away her body for a simple necklace and who, to keep from catching the king's measles, "isolated" herself at the Trianon for several days with three or four noblemen, without her servants or ladies-in-waiting! Of course, this "quarantine" stirred up quite a scandal, inspiring any number of jokes about the respective "fevers" of the royal couple (some gossips even went so far as to imply that the king's pox were due to the queen's dalliances).

We would continue our walk beneath elders, laurels, and redbuds. I warn the Marquise to take care that her ravishing dress does not snag upon the raspberry canes and extend my arm. We arrive in the refreshing grotto—the Marquise is a bit warm after such a long walk in her corset. The spot is ideal—cool and shady—and the interior of the grotto the perfect harmony of nature and artifice. A bench seems to be sculpted out of the rock itself but has been covered with a mossy fabric to protect the queen from the damp when she comes here to read for hours on end. Not that I doubt Marie Antoinette's virtues, but it seems unlikely that one would read in such a place—it's quite simply too dark! And besides, the queen prefers that others read to her; yet she comes here alone. This is clearly a refuge. A gently bubbling fountain in the depths of the grotto covers the sound of conversation…and the grotto is equipped with two entrances and hidden by a rock formation, a peephole. The queen could wait and watch who was coming without being seen herself, and if need be, shoo her visitors out the other entrance. What happens next between the beautiful marquise and me, will of course, remain a mystery. But a final word before leaving Marie Antoinette's grotto: it was sitting on the bench in her "little house of moss" that the queen first learned the Revolution had begun.

Marie Antoinette remains a legendary figure of Versailles. I think that only Princess Diana managed to overshadow her in the hearts of the French. The two women had certain points in common—both embody the myth of a princess of the people who died too young. To me, Marie Antoinette symbolizes the feminine character of the gardens at Versailles. When I look at the extreme gentleness that characterizes her portrait by Louise Elisabeth Vigée Le Brun, I think that Marie Antoinette knew how to make herself loved as much as hated. One only has to see how those who knew her, particularly women, talked about her— of course, one must allow for flattery and nostalgia, but fifteen or twenty years after the Revolution, such literary deference was no longer necessary in writing about the monarchy. The writings of Madame Vigée Le Brun are particularly touching. More than admiration, one senses a real bond had formed between the two women. In the case of one of her portraits of the queen, Vigée Le Brun recounts how her own advancing pregnancy made it impossible for her to paint for a scheduled sitting. Far from taking offense, Marie Antoinette came in person to inquire into her health, and the following day, when a new sitting had been decided upon, the thoughtful queen came to her portraitist's aid, picking up a brush that had fallen to the ground: the queen lowering herself before her pregnant servant. There is gentleness and friendship in this gesture, something very touching and feminine. I believe that Marie Antoinette was sincere when she played at being a shepherdess in her Hamlet—just a poor country girl from Austria in search of simplicity. In truth, this simplicity was the greatest of luxuries at the court of Versailles—one for which she was reproached long afterwards—so much so that in 1854, the Goncourt brothers saw "this liberty, this offhandedness, this abandonment of the essential dogmas of royal etiquette"[7] as one of the causes of the regime's fall.

For me, Marie Antoinette is the fairy godmother of Versailles. Many women inspired the creation of these gardens—they would be nothing without the influence of Madame de Montespan, and especially Madame de Pompadour—but Marie Antoinette did even more. Not only did she have the king replant and modify the gardens of Versailles, she put her mark on the choices that were made. One may speak of Louis XIV's labyrinth, but it is the Queen's Hamlet.

After all these royal anecdotes, its time to turn to a story from the Revolution. (I apologize in advance, for it will be sad.) The revolutionaries were not gentle with Versailles, neither the château nor the gardens. Although its destruction was avoided, the château was an unpleasant symbol of the monarchy just

---

7. Edmond and Jules de Goncourt, *La Société française pendant la Révolution,* 1854.

outside the gates of Paris. Still, its relative distance from Paris had made it the object of rumors, which were only aggravated by those who had fallen out of favor at court. Versailles concentrated the essence of the people's animosity, and nothing is as unifying in troubled times as a common object of hatred. The revolutionaries stormed the palace hoping for riches only to find the empty coffers of a state in dire straits. This was all it took to stir up rage and transform the "visitors" into vandals. In the Tuileries, the sansculottes slashed the queen's bed, and at Versailles, they carted off all they could carry. The remaining furnishings were seized and later sold off at auction. The château and the gardens owe their lives to the gardener Richard. The grounds were to be divided up into cultivable fields, which would have destroyed the domain—Versailles would have likely suffered the same fate as many other châteaux in France had Richard not had the idea to plant vegetables and fruit trees to feed the local population. Beyond this practical, even vital role, it was a rightful turning of tables in the eyes of the commoners. Paris had long supplied Versailles with men, knowledge, and talent; it was now up to Versailles to save Paris from famine…(and Richard from the gallows!) Indeed, the blood spilled by the sansculottes was not always blue. The personnel of Versailles paid a heavy price in the Revolution. Such was the fate of Richard Mique, the architect of Marie Antoinette's grotto. Denounced by his own daughter, he and his son were accused of treason. In times of crisis, family bonds don't always grow stronger.

Among the victims of the revolutionary era, one finds the names of two survivors, Marion and Jean de l'Eau, both of whom figure in the *Tales and Legends of the Trianon*. Marion was the daughter of one of the gardeners, and the queen had taken a liking to her. Although Marie Antoinette is often portrayed as a tyrant and spendthrift, her love of children has never been called into question. The little Marion was about twelve on the eve of the Revolution. Children worked in those days, and Marion's task was to cut roses for the queen's bouquets— the queen herself probably also dreamed of "playing the florist." Neither she nor the little Marion missed a daily meeting. It is even said that at the beginning of the Revolution, during the short-lived constitutional monarchy, Marie Antoinette was brought to tears when she heard the teenage Marion singing revolutionary songs. This detail is probably untrue, but it certainly adds to the story! There was a great deal of weeping in the eighteenth century, and Marie Antoinette certainly had reason to cry. But it was Marion who would sob when her queen was carted off to prison. She wasn't the only one in mourning. Jean de l'Eau, who got his name because he was entrusted with fetching the queen's spring water in Ville-d'Avray, enrolled in the army to defend the Revolution, which was now threatened from beyond France's borders. Jean was forced to leave Marion, whom he had loved in secret.

A few years later, Marion was chosen to embody the goddess of Reason in the grand atheistic celebrations of the Terror.

She was expected to sing the glories of the Republic on a parade float in a pseudo-antique costume that was nearly transparent. This was too much for the modest and devout Marion. What was she to do? If she refused, she knew that neither she nor her family would escape the hungry guillotine. In desperation, she took a bouquet of roses, the same she had always made with such talent, and plunged her face into the thorns. A disfigured and bloody goddess of Reason was out of the question—Marion, thanks to her roses, had escaped the humiliating parade.

Jean de l'Eau returned from war, in which he had lost an arm, but not his love for Marion. Still, he was sure that she would never want him in such a state. But, in the end, love triumphed over all. At this point you've discovered that gardeners also have a sentimental side. We aren't alone. This revolutionary fairy tale continued well into the Empire. Napoleon was so touched by the story that he ennobled Jean de l'Eau and named him the head gardener of the Trianon, where he worked for more than fifty years. Marion spent the rest of her life in the château, among the roses she had always loved.

And today? The garden is still the setting of stories that range from the tragic to the sordid, as well as, happily, to the comic. We contemporaries have our own fairy tales. I remember when one of the guards rushed into my office at seven thirty in the morning, looking haggard and terrified. Usually square jawed and proud in his military uniform, he was not the sort of man given over to fantasy. Yet, that morning, he looked as though he had seen a ghost—eyes popping out of his head and pale, he was still shaking when I asked him what had happened. Ashamed, but without the slightest hint of irony, he announced that there were ghosts in one of the lakes of the Trianon. A few minutes later, we headed out the door together, in search of the paranormal. The sight that met our eyes was certainly unusual—in the beautiful July morning light, two blond young women, completely nude, were playing in the clear waters of the lake. There was indeed something otherworldly about the scene. For a few moments I wanted to believe that the grace of those two nymphs was something supernatural. But reality is always in a hurry for a return to order—our nymphs weren't long in noticing our presence and started exclaiming to each other in a guttural language before running to take refuge in a tent that, fascinated as we had been, neither the guard nor I had noticed until then. The mermaids turned out to be Dutch tourists who intentionally had gotten stuck in the park after closing. After a night in their tent, they had decided to take a quick bath, like they did every morning, in one of the most beautiful bathtubs of the world. The poor guard's sanity was secure and, in spite of myself, I directed the nymphs to a nearby campground.

The 1980s were full of stories of people shut in the park after closing. We had fewer personnel at our disposition, and I believe it was a fad to spend the night in a public place such as a museum, a park, a monument, or a school—it had become a rite of passage. Today, between the special visits on France's

Heritage Days, the weekly extended evening hours in museums, and the annual all-night art festivals of the *Nuits blanches*, the experience must have lost its flavor of transgression. The night is no longer synonymous with the prohibited and the intimate, just with long lines and overcrowded spaces bathed in a painfully official and modish atmosphere.

Still, not everybody who gets shut in the park does so on purpose. I'm sure that one Japanese tourist, in particular, would have willingly forgone the entire experience. The Queen's Hamlet was, in those days, inhabited by a caretaker. He didn't talk much, and lived there alone, without a wife or children. Still, his jolly beard and round face were hardly a terrifying sight.

It was a cold and damp winter evening of the sort that I like, and a thick fog had enveloped the grounds. Night falls quickly at that time of the year and a Japanese woman, daydreaming, had gotten lost and found herself alone. The poor thing was shivering with cold and fear, and for good reason—the gardens were empty, poorly lit, and the nocturnal wildlife was on the prowl. The slightest noise echoed through the silence. It was the time of night when the statues seem to look at you. I only walk in the gardens at that hour if I want to give myself a scare. I like a little thrill, and if I'm in the mood, I know just where to go. The Basin of the Four Nymphs is the gloomiest spot in the dusk twilight. Just a short distance from the Grand Trianon, this part of the slope is invisible, unless one stands on the balustrades of the terrace, as is the rest of the park, which sits on slightly higher ground. This is one of the rare spots in the garden where one is invisible, in the sense that, although the gardens are full of hiding places where you won't be seen, the places where you become invisible in spite of yourself are rare. You can hide in a bosquet, but at the Basin of the Four Nymphs, you can't be seen. And no matter what happens to you, there won't be a witness. This is one of the reasons that this part of the grounds is so carefully watched over by the gardeners when the park is open. The lost tourist continued down the main allée and luckily ended up at the Trianon. She saw a light in the distance. She cautiously approached the Hamlet, and knocked on the door, hoping her frightening experience had come to an end, only to find herself face to face with a man, knife in hand, eyes wide, and his shirt covered in blood. She screamed and fainted on the spot, only to awake in the caretaker's bed, surrounded by the friends who had come to share a suckling pig with him… The poor woman probably didn't return to Versailles, and the caretaker was known as "The Ogre" for the rest of his days.

Although the gardens aren't dangerous today, this wasn't always the case. Closing the park at night and restricting automobile traffic has kept it from becoming the sort of open-air sex market that is the Bois de Boulogne. Without a car, it's harder to hide or to expose oneself, and most of all, much harder to get away. Cars and nature are never a good match, believe me. But at the same time, it would be unfair to blame cars for the various sorts of pollution that have affected the gardens in the past.

At the risk of shattering the myths about the superior morals of the aristocracy, it was without doubt under the monarchy that the allées of Versailles were their most dangerous. There was the assassination attempt against Louis XV, of course, and later the Affair of the Diamond Necklace, but the gardens were already perilous in the time of Louis XIV—mugging, theft, poaching, and even the murder of creatures other than the deer—so much so that the gardens were enclosed and watched over by armed guards at night. They carried pistols—rather rare in those days—whose bullets had been blessed by the clergy.

Today Versailles fears neither swordfights nor gunshots, but the effects of mental illness are still a regular presence. The strong symbolic, even mythical, value attached to the château and to royalty is probably the cause of this, and the gardens do seem to attract the mentally unbalanced. In thirty-plus years I've seen uncountable numbers of Louis XIVs and Marie Antoinettes, a fair number of Napoleons, a few Madame de Maintenons, a Mozart, a Mansart, and a Frederick the Great, who had shown up at the wrong palace. This gentle form of insanity is an excellent indicator of a historical figure's popularity. Although it amuses me from afar, I don't like to run into it in person. I still remember the woman who came to my quarters at the Trianon. She was a small person, in her forties, with short graying hair pulled back at the temples with little black barrettes used on children. She was so plain that at first I thought she was one of the many nuns who made the rounds asking for donations to the local hospital. But she didn't wear a cross and her lost and desperate appearance hardly fit the description of a nun.

When I opened the door, she spoke to me in a peremptory tone.

"Monsieur, what are you doing in my house?"

I always feel a bit guilty for the privilege of living on the grounds, and almost involuntarily, I began trying to justify myself, explaining that it was an official apartment owned by the state, and that, although I was living in it for the time being, it was only because the previous tenant had been forced to move…Soon, I was lost in my explanations, only to hear her reply, with the extreme courtesy that the insane often have.

"I'm very sorry, you see, Monsieur, and please don't think that I doubt your words or intentions, but you are in my home."

I suddenly realized what was happening and decided to play along. In spite of myself I had gotten caught up.

Since Molière had slept in the house, I exclaimed, "Madeleine Béjart!"

She looked offended and I shivered, thinking how the good man Molière had ended up marrying the daughter of his mistress Madeleine, Armande. Even though this woman had lost all touch with reality, I had no desire to offend her. But she continued:

"I have nothing to do with that clown! You can see quite well that I'm Madame de Pompadour. Let me in."

And as she spoke these words, she began to cry.

I decided to take her to the nurse's station, but her parents crossed paths with us at the gates of the Trianon. "La petite" had been allowed to go out that weekend, and her aging mother and father had thought that shock might be good for her. Besides, their daughter had always wanted to see Versailles.

The gardens have their little dramas. Some can be told in a sentence, like the episode of the alcoholic camel that Louis XVI brought to the Ménagerie, only for it to die of grief. Others could fill volumes.

# THE DREAMER
≋≋≋≋≋≋≋≋≋≋≋≋≋≋

I AM A dreamer. A day doesn't go by that I don't wonder at the beauty of a flower, a majestic tree, or the gentle light that filters through the leaves in the forest of the Grand Parc at the end of the day.

Often, I even chat with my trees. In the past, when I had my share of worries, after the crowds of visitors had left the gardens, I enjoyed sitting at the foot of a massive beech tree and talking to myself, the wooden colossus as my only witness. The trees of Versailles know more about me than my closest friends and family.

The tree bears witness to all that happens, to all that is said and left unsaid. The tree knows, sees, and hears all, but betrays nobody; it is sensitive to our joy as well as our grief. I know my silent friend will keep my secrets to the grave, just as he has for all those before me who came to confide their pain and sorrow.

I've never thought I was very good looking and I'm some-times bothered by my baldness. But the bald cypress is another story—with pride, it wears a name that brings shame to men. The name of the parasol pine indicates both its form and function. I, who so hate being known as "Alain the gardener," ought to fol-low their example. I don't mind being referred to as a gardener;

it's seeing my name stuck onto my profession that bothers me. "Nicolas the gardener," "Michel the gardener," and "Hubert the gardener" have become media figures in France. But why do we have to be so familiar? Are people referred to as "Jules the plumber," "Henry the carpenter," or "Melanie the hairdresser"?

My father and my grandfather were both called Baraton. Our family tree shows that "Baraton" used to be "Baraton de la Vergne." I appreciate this detail not so much for the aristocratic sound of the full name, but because *vergne* means "wood" in old French. In my eyes, a name with hints of predestination is much more evocative than dull old "Alain the gardener." The tree knows nothing of noble French names with "de" or "de la" holding them together. The world of plants could care less about the artifice that gives certain humans a feeling of superiority. Just as connected to its roots as to its offshoots, the tree isn't concerned by its origins alone: it grows on both ends of its being.

It was botanists who first named many plants, and behind those names, whether common or scientific, there often lies a story. The magnolia was named in homage to the director of the Montpellier Botanical Garden, Pierre Magnol. Did he imagine, when he died at the age of seventy-seven, that one of our most beautiful trees would come to carry his name? Anders Dahl brought the dahlia back from Mexico, and the Jesuit priest Georg Josef Kamel, who left France to study the flora of the Philippines, gave his name to the romantic camellia. The wife of François I loved the plums that ripened in the royal orchards and

encouraged their development. To thank the queen, the growers named a particularly sweet and juicy variety Reine Claude.
The tribute later caused problems during the Revolution when
all symbols of monarchy were tracked down and eliminated.
The statues of saints on church facades were decapitated, and
in Parisian markets during the terror, it took courage to ask the
tradesmen for Reine Claude plums or even for simple daisies,
known to the French as Reines-Marguerites.

Botanists were often odd characters. Capable of telling apart
two plants that seemed nearly identical, they classified and defined
the characteristics of trees previously unknown to them. By simply
observing the parts of a flower, they were able to explain how plants
reproduced as well as the characteristics of their growth. To me,
these men were geniuses. Men of science, they Latinized their ter-
minology, both to keep their knowledge to themselves and to communicate with scientists who spoke other languages. Almost por-
nographic when compared to uncultured moralists, they compared
humans and plants down to the most intimate details. Orchids, for
example, often have swollen bulblike stems that resemble olives.
Had they been prudes, botanists might have made reference to
the Latin *Olea* for olive in composing the orchid's name. Instead,
they preferred *Orkhis*, Greek for testicle.

Trees provide a way for me to travel in time and around the
world, using the gardens of Versailles as a form of transporta-
tion. When I water my bougainvillea, I think of Louis-Antoine
de Bougainville, a man who sailed the seven seas. Perhaps he

had the pleasure of conversing with the great Cherokee chief Sequoia, who invented an alphabet to better communicate with the Europeans who lost little time in killing off his people. Not even oceans stop intolerance. On the continent where the learned Cherokee once lived, the giant sequoias seem to supplicate the gods with their branches, on behalf of the populations that once respected them. Considered sacred, they survived the centuries, and even today, are protected by law.

I also think of Richelieu, Louis XIII's austere but farsighted minister who already, in 1629, taxed the tobacco and coffee produced in the Trianon's greenhouses. In the summertime gardens, I imagine the sublime nymph Daphne transforming into a laurel tree to escape the insatiable Apollo. In the early spring, I think of Hyacinth, who, thanks to the same god, became the flower that perfumes our parterres. The brook in the Queen's Hamlet reminds me of Narcissus, who was also transformed into a flower. The gods had a strange habit of turning themselves and others into plants!

High walls shelter the Trianon's nursery, where we raise trees and shrubs, and in the fall, pick kiwis. The story of this fruit, which comes from China, is a strange one. The kiwi was introduced in New Zealand in 1906, where it adapted well to the climate, allowing for a profitable production. In the 1970s, the kiwi growers of New Zealand wanted to target foreign markets but didn't know how to conquer the United States. It was difficult to sell a fruit that was known as the "Chinese gooseberry" in the middle of the Cold War. It was out of the question to sell anything in the United States that might be associated with China, a bastion of communism. Uncle Sam was determined not to taste the forbidden fruit! Advertisers rebaptized the politically incorrect gooseberry "kiwi" in honor of the emblematic bird of New Zealand, where the fruit was grown. The operation was a success: the gods of marketing, while less romantic than those of antiquity, had managed to transform a fruit not into a graceful nymph, but into a rather ugly bird.

Plants, it has been shown time and again, make us better people. Being near trees calms the anxious. The daily walk of the hospitalized usually takes place in the gardens surrounding the medical center, and it is enough to visit on a rainy day to see the disappointment of the ill, deprived of their flowers and chlorophyll. Plants soothe our spirits, and sometimes prove themselves veritable benefactors of humanity. In 1532, the conquistadors discovered a strange plant, which they packed into their ships and brought back to Europe. The plant was grown for its flowers but interested few until, two centuries later, the nutritious qualities of its tubers were rediscovered: the potato was born! Easy to grow and conserve, it improved the daily lives of man, and, for a time, saved the poor of Ireland from famine, until, a few years later, the potato crop was struck by a fungus that led to famine again. Entire villages left Ireland for the United States. Among the immigrants were the Clinton, Reagan, and Kennedy families. The fungus changed the course of world history. Who knows? If it had struck China, Mandarin might be the official language of New York. The trees in the Queen's Hamlet knew this period—they were among the first to watch Monsieur Parmentier, France's celebrated champion of the potato as food, conversing with Louis XVI.

I often imagine what our lives would be like without trees. We won't even dwell on the fact that our atmosphere would be sorely lacking in oxygen. To hunt and eat game, our ancestors needed spears. The discovery of iron was crucial, but imagine a weapon without a handle! The prey was consumed cooked— but without wood, there is no fire. The tree gave human beings everything, but today it has received little in the way of thanks. On the contrary, trees are too often massacred, cut down, or vandalized. I like my trees and I protect them, keeping watch to make sure they lack nothing. I observe with concern when they fall sick and dread the day I will have to order them cut down. The gardener plants trees; he doesn't like to cut them—it is the lumberjack that attacks their poor trunks. The dead thud of a tree falling to the earth and making it shake tells me that a story is over. Of course, another will take its place, but it won't have the strength or beauty of its predecessor for another hundred years.

Marie Antoinette's mighty oak once stood at the entrance to the Trianon, remembering all the glorious and painful moments of the gardens. From the top of its 115 feet, it watched all the other trees that grow in the gardens as they first arrived. It heard the king converse with Le Nôtre and mourned the loss of a young queen, condemned to an unjust death. It wondered about the bored Napoleon's impatient pacing. It was born in 1681 and died during the drought of the summer of 2003.

Happily, a venerable old oak still stands not far from the Trianon. The oldest in the gardens, it was born at the end of the seventeenth century, but it is not found on any map and has remained completely unknown to those who make a living talking about Versailles and its gardens. Far from the vandals and the noise of the château, it lives a discreet life. This nameless oak is magnificent and in good health. It seems to respond to La Fontaine's exclamation before the gardens, "May they last a thousand years."

I have any number of photos of Marie Antoinette's oak—with its leaves, in the autumn, standing tall and lying on the ground. But the most precious souvenir of that tree that accompanied almost forty years of my life is a modest leaf, pressed and dry between the pages of an old book on botany. Rousseau's herbarium contained the thousands of plants collected in Alpine meadows. Mine is far more modest, but precious all the same. A leaf from a tree that I loved and that returned to the Garden of Eden where now dwell Le Nôtre, Richard, La Fontaine, and Molière, as well as all of the anonymous gardeners who have preceded me. May they rest in peace beneath its branches.

# LE NÔTRE AND THE REST OF US
≈≈≈≈≈≈≈≈≈≈≈≈≈≈≈≈≈≈≈≈≈≈≈≈≈≈≈≈≈≈≈≈≈≈≈≈≈

A TREE IS an anonymous work of art. Gardeners know this and don't expect to be remembered by posterity for their work. (They do, however, fight against those who would carve names into the trunks of their darlings.) Even the most famous gardener of all had a name that was collective: *Le Nôtre* literally means "ours" in French. The rest of us gardeners shouldn't struggle against being forgotten—it wouldn't be right if we of all people were afraid of returning to the earth. We also have our great men, our heroes, but an excess of modesty (another common trait of the trade) or perhaps just the calm capacity to accept disappearance has left many of us absent from history. Today, people come to visit the grounds where Louis XIV, Saint-Simon, Colbert, and Napoleon once walked, but not the gardens of La Quintinie and Richard. I'd like to try to fix this injustice and create something new: a family tree of gardeners.

Doctors have Asclepius; poets, Apollo; and gardeners, André Le Nôtre. He makes for a strange ancestor. He left us no writings, not even a single letter—his entire posterity is composed of wood and leaves, not ink and paper. Is this itself a sign? Perhaps this is the reason many gardeners don't like to leave anything behind.

Unlike his personality, his life is not entirely unknown. A good gardener, son and grandson of gardeners, he was born in the spring, in the month of March, the season when we plant tuberose bulbs in the cool earth, and when crocuses and tulips poke their noses from the dirt. André wasn't found in a cabbage patch, but in the heart of Paris, at the Tuileries Palace where his father, Jean, shared the responsibility of creating the royal gardens with Claude Mollet. The young André had quite the "precedents" as they say in medicine and law: his grandfather, Pierre, had also been in charge of the parterres at the Tuileries since 1572. Heredity, in those days, was a heavy burden or benefit, as trades functioned through guilds and apprenticeships to the point that one's professional fate was more or less sealed from birth. Nobody asked their children what they were going to be when they grew up. André was born on the right side of the wall—positions and trades were passed down from generation to generation. But these traditions were not always followed: Molière was supposed to have become a weaver, Racine a clerk. At most, the next generation's occupations might be adjusted to their tastes—Jean Le Nôtre must have preferred drawing to raking and therefore became the garden's draftsman.

His son, however, wanted to become a painter. Jean had nothing against this—developing a sense of color and line couldn't hurt a developing young gardener, particularly when he was destined to succeed him as the draftsman of the Tuileries's parterres. What was more, the young André had talent—doubtlessly inherited from his father. Who knows? Maybe his father wanted to become a painter as well—talent is rarely suppressed for more than two generations. André went to the Louvre, which in those days wasn't a museum but a workshop, where he studied with the portraitist Simon Vouet. A great traveler who had visited all of the capitals of Europe from London to Constantinople, Vouet had been given the daunting task of establishing a National Style in the face of the splendors of Rome and Rubens. He succeeded—an emulator of Caravaggio in the land of Descartes. I can imagine the young Le Nôtre walking through the immense halls of the Louvre, devouring the luminous lines of his master's paintings. It may be that the roots of Le Nôtre's aesthetic can be found in Vouet's clean, sensual subjects. The gardener's taste for statuary and its alliance with nature is strikingly similar to the way the painter treats figures—their pale, sculptural forms standing out against dark leafy backgrounds. Le Nôtre's love of painting can, in any case, be traced back to his youth—a passionate admirer of Poussin and Claude Lorrain, he surrounded himself with one of the greatest art collections of his time. At the end of his life he gave it all to Louis XIV in person! The collection contained a sufficient number of masterpieces for such a gesture not to seem ridiculous to a man who saw the *Mona Lisa* every night when he went to bed. A few of these paintings still hang in the Louvre, and they give an idea of the aesthetic finesse of our great gardener ancestor. None of them are paintings of gardens; in fact, the vegetal is particularly absent—but what lines, what perspective! Poussin's *Christ and the* Woman Taken in Adultery almost seems an homage to the laws of optics and geometry, whereas all of Claude Lorrain's *Seaport at Sunset* glows and leads the eye to the distant, shining horizon. In this second painting, I can see the Le Nôtre of Versailles's Grand Canal. If you stand on the terrace across from the Bassin de Latone at dawn or dusk—depending on your taste and lifestyle—the water, fountains, and marble all catch, reflect and diffract the light, which seems to fill the space and lead the gaze to the limits of the perspective where sun is condensing its energy before being swallowed up by the gardens. Motionless in contemplation, you have become one of those tiny figures in the paintings of Claude Gellée, *dit* "le Lorrain."

Geometry entered the world of painting during the Quattrocento: triangles compose the foundation of da Vinci's faces and, in the artist's most famous drawing, man himself stands in the perfection of the circle. What was more natural than to continue by plotting out that same geometry on earth, starting with gardens? Before, gardens had been simply arranged in squares for the purpose of producing fruits and vegetables. At the beginning of the seventeenth century, Jacques Boyceau de la Barauderie wrote in his *Treatise of Gardening According to the Laws of Nature and Art*, "I have grown quite weary of gardens always divided up using straight lines and squares, either into nine or sixteen sections. I would like to see something else."

This "something else" so desired by Louis XIII's gardener was secretly being plotted in the corridors of the Louvre. It was there that Le Nôtre learned the rudiments of the French Baroque: clear, orderly, and sensual. It was also there that he met Le Brun, a fellow student in the school of Simon Vouet. The seventeenth century had its Capitoline Triad of Racine, Corneille, and Molière, but it also had a more plebian triad, educated at the Louvre in the 1630s—a trio of "Le's" composed of Le Brun, Le Vau, and Le Nôtre.

Our glorious gardening ancestor was not a fanciful dreamer. I even suspect he was something of a social climber, although it is hard to blame him for being so in a century so marked by ambition. At the age of only twenty-two he was named head gardener to Monsieur, the king's brother. Gaston d'Orléans was a great lover of gardens and entrusted Le Nôtre with the grounds of the Palais de Luxembourg. Here, Le Nôtre multiplied the vegetal lace and embroidery, along with, in my opinion, a fair amount of sycophancy, and in 1637, he succeeded his father at the Tuileries. The young man had proved himself and was now ready to take the next step. In 1640 he married Françoise Langlois, the daughter of an ordinary artillery captain. The young couple moved into an attractive residence at the Tuileries, where Le Nôtre was finally given the room for his own secret garden—or at least a private one. In the narrow space allotted to him, Le Nôtre managed to cram in forty oleanders, two pomegranates, and fourteen orange trees trimmed into topiary globes—creating a little piece of the Italy that he had yet to visit but which was the subject of every conversation, most especially those of his painter friends for whom travel to the land of Botticelli and Dante had become a quasi-obligatory rite of passage. Since the arrival of Catherine de Medici, French culture had been imported from across the Alps—artists aspired to reproduce the Italian style, with the daring of them attempting to renew Italian art through variations *à la française*—but this was as far as their innovations went. To this point Le Nôtre had done all an ambitious young man of twenty-five was capable of—he had served, pleased, and conformed enough to be called a "brilliant young man" by his elders. The only shadow on the faultless career path of this young virtuoso was that none of his issue survived childhood. His heritage would not be human.

Louis XIII died in 1643, providing the opportunity for changes in the palace hierarchy. Le Nôtre used the occasion to become the draftsman of the royal gardens that same year. In 1646 he redrew the parterre of the Queen's Garden at Fontainbleau, with broad rectangular plantings of trees in allées, complex geometrical forms, and the deep, dark green of boxwood. The "Le Nôtre style" was starting to take shape and the queen was delighted with the results. No further obstacle lay in the path of his becoming the leading gardener in the kingdom of France, but he would go much further than this, making France the leading kingdom of gardens. His success was so great that all the provincial nobles wanted their own garden by Le Nôtre, or if they didn't have the means (Monsieur didn't work for peanuts), at least a garden à la Le Nôtre. Rich financiers bought châteaux in the countryside surrounding Paris and sank colossal fortunes into their landscaping; Le Nôtre was present on every site.

Shortly after the Fronde, Fouquet, France's Superintendent of Finances and a brilliant schemer and aesthete, brought together the big three of construction. Le Vau, the architect recently (in 1657) named general controller of the king's construction projects, was in charge of the project, in which he was assisted by Le Brun and Le Nôtre. The new château was a godsend to the three men—Fouquet was extremely rich, a complete megalomaniac, and a great lover and connoisseur of the arts. Moreover, he had the intelligence to trust his artists, imposing no budget, aesthetic limit, or deadline. A more ideal patron of the arts had not been known since Lorenzo de' Medici. The three men were old collaborators and friends—the idea of working together again on the same project must have excited them. The amplitude of the site was also glorious—with nearly a hundred acres of gardens, Vaux-le-Vicomte was without a doubt the largest construction project in France at the time. Freedom, friendship, wealth, and space to realize one's ideas: what more could one want? The grandeur of the situation turned the talented young men into visionaries. Faced with the complex shape of the site, Le Nôtre had the idea of adapting his design to the terrain, using its topography instead of working against it and employing the new optical laws and the art of trompe l'œil he had learned under the tutelage of Simon Vouet. He worked with the slope and rechanneled the local rivers to obtain a perspective that opened up across nearly two miles. The castle felt as though it ruled over a sober, voluntarily denuded landscape. Boxwood tracery, very few flowers, and design took priority over color, and with great refinement. The motifs in the parterres went so far as to recall the figures of Ottoman carpets—in Le Nôtre's hands, nature became docile and malleable, a medium that the artist could shape according to his desires. The forms of the parterres were so impeccably trimmed that they seemed to have been carved from green marble—"I hate movement, it deforms the line," our glorious gardening ancestor might have said, had he been a bit more talkative. Still, the triumph of order still hides a few surprises—the grottos, which seem to be situated on either side of a rectangular lake, give the impression that they are farther and farther away as one approaches them. As viewers continue forward, they discover a long, silver canal, previously invisible, that now crosses the perspective at the end of which lie the two grottos that initially seemed so close. An uninformed eye might even think they had moved!

Order and surprise—the essence of the French Baroque in a nutshell, thriving and green on a few acres owned by a rich statesman. People were not yet using the term *jardin à la française* but Le Nôtre's style had been born. Visitors flocked to marvel at the sober parterres, the spare grandeur of the canal, and the mirrorlike reflections of the basins. Everyone agreed that the result was royal. La Fontaine, another artistic protégé of Fouquet, described the château in his poem "Le Songe de Vaux":

*In a dream, he revealed a magnificent palace*
*With grottos, canals, a superb portico,*
*Places, the beauty of which*
*I might have thought enchanted,*
*If Vaux was not part of this world:*
*They were such that the Sun's*
*Rays revealed*
*nothing so worthy as Vaux.*[8]

This was more than enough to attract the ire of a young king with a rather dark character. (I've already mentioned Fouquet's fate.) As Voltaire put it, "On August 17 at six in the evening, Fouquet was the king of France, and at two the following morning, he was nothing." Hardly had the party ended than Fouquet and all of his possessions were seized. Nobody could rival the Sun King's glory with impunity. Having flown too high, Icarus burned his wings. A last word on the wealthy, unfortunate Fouquet: during the twenty years of prison to which he had been condemned, the deposed superintendent received a single visit—from his gardener. All of his other "friends" abandoned him, fearing the king's reaction. Le Nôtre, who only made one visit, still took the time to remember his former benefactor.

Kings don't always behave like proper princes. For the first time in the history of France, the head of state used his power

---

8. Translator's note: The conjugation of the French verb *valoir*, "to be worth," is a homophone with the word "Vaux," creating a bit of wordplay.

to increase a punishment instead of reducing it. Fouquet was condemned to prison for life. With his former superintendent locked away, Louis XIV pillaged Vaux-le-Vicomte, carrying off every last candlestick and bedsheet before sequestering the château. Fouquet's wife had her own fortune, which the king had no right to take. When she bought the château back with her own money, the king, unable to dispossess her, sent her into exile—his pettiness and injustice were of royal proportions. Le Brun, Le Nôtre, Le Vau, and La Fontaine—Vaux's entire artistic team— were seized along with the furniture.

When I'm on the Island of Oléron, I often watch children build sandcastles and notice their mix of tenderness and circumspection. Tyrannical and clumsy, they build alone, and it isn't rare to see the shovel strike if another tiny despot dares construct in the same vicinity. Louis XIV was twenty-four when he decided to begin working on Versailles—and although he was no longer a clumsy child, he intended to build his castle on sandy ground. "Versailles, the most thankless of places, without wood, water, or earth. Almost everything is shifting sand or airless marshland, and cannot be good," noted Saint-Simon. For the acid-tongued memorialist the young king's calamitous decision was born only from the "superb pleasure of forcing nature." It was Le Nôtre who had the brilliant idea of building the Grand Canal to drain the marsh. He plotted out lines of perspective, the shapes of the lakes, the parterres, and the bosquets, transforming the mud of Versailles into a fantastic Hanging Garden of Babylon that Le

Brun populated with majestic statuary. The gardener could do as he pleased and had colossal means with which to do so—he magnified and perfected the aesthetic of Vaux-le-Vicomte, adding the note of excess that is the mark of masterpiece. The broad, spare axes alternated with the secret world of the bosquets, teeming with fantastical sculptures, treasures, and fountains. The Ballroom, the *Berceau d'eau*, the Salle des Festins, the Encelade, and the Labyrinth—the garden's countless surprises lay in wait for the court's admiration and amusement. Each bosquet revealed a new atmosphere, a new feeling of time, a new story, so that every stroll was an overwhelming experience, in which everything seemed to be mixed up—beginning with fiction and reality. Movement and line entered into dialogue without their actual materials taking on the slightest importance—fountains, plants, and marble were at once sinuous and harmonious. The experience of the garden was overwhelming because of the way in which it played with the profound nature of the elements—water, plants, and stone were no longer limited to their basic characteristics, but instead exchanged and combined the same lines and motifs. The seventeenth century brought to life the classical tragedy and its violent passions by using the poetic constraint of the alexandrine meter and the rule of the three Aristotelian unities. To me, Le Nôtre's garden is the vegetal equivalent of this mastery: an incredible exercise in style constrained by rules of form. The park itself often played the role of decor—in this sense, the art of scenography is by no means a contemporary concept.

The result was a triumph. The nobility clamored to come to Versailles and admire its park as much as the château. Le Nôtre's projects multiplied, notably at Fontainebleau and Saint-Germain. The sumptuous promenade of the terrace at Saint-Germain is the mark of another sort of progress—its slight misalignment makes it possible to admire both the view and the landscaping. Le Nôtre brought greater nuance to his rigor. Paris was not left untouched either. Abandoning gardens, he extended the Tuileries with the Avenue du Roule and an eight-branched star, today better known as the Champs-Elysées. A generous prince, Louis XIV sometimes "lent out" his gardener-genius—to Condé, returned from exile, for whom Le Nôtre designed Chantilly, and to Colbert, for whom he created the Parc des Sceaux. His renown became international, and he created the Saint James's Park for Charles II of England. Versailles was to be enlarged and, remaining faithful to the man who had guaranteed his success, Louis XIV again entrusted the project to Le Nôtre, who created the park of the Trianon and, at the other end of the town, the gardens at Clagny (which no longer exist), destined for the king's illegitimate children. Saint-Cloud, Meudon, Noisy, Maintenon, the Nouveau Trianon, and Marly, with its famous river, were soon added to the list. The king's own glory merged with that of his humble gardener.

There was no lack of critics at the time, however. Marly was the object of a certain amount of mockery. Saint-Simon could not help but condemn "the King's bad taste in all things, and the

superb pleasure he takes in forcing nature, that neither the cost-
liest war nor religious devotion manage to blunt." The aristocracy
was both jealous and cowardly. Saint-Simon forgot to mention,
however, that in Le Nôtre's hands, the former "haunt of serpents
and carrion, toads and frogs" had become a jewel—what was
more natural to a gardener than to turn mud into gold? For having given our profession its letters of nobility, Le Nôtre is our
greatest forefather. Louis XIV was well aware of this, deciding in
1675 to ennoble his gardener, a rare honor indeed—but after all,
wasn't nobility something born of the land?

One story is especially dear to me. It is said that the king was
always pushing Le Nôtre to hurry up with his various projects,
who in turn responded with his humble humor, "I'm not the slow
one, it's nature." When it came time to choose his coat of arms,
he asked that it be decorated with three snails, a cabbage, a rake,
and a spade. "How could I forget my spade, thanks to which your
Majesty has honored me with so much kindness?" A fitting close
to Le Nôtre's own fable, that of the King and the Gardener.

It seems strange that such an arrogant and inflexible king
could show so much equanimity, but Louis XIV always protected
his gardener. When he was in Italy, Le Nôtre was introduced to
the Pope. Confused and uninformed as to the holy etiquette, he
could think of nothing better to do than kissing the Holy Father.
News of the kiss soon reached France and it became as famous
as that of Judas. The old gardener was the laughingstock of the
court. One was allowed to possess vice at Versailles, but this did

not include seeming foolish. Like Le Nôtre, Louis XIV was a man of few words, and little wit. Still, he defended his protégé and friend, remarking, "I kiss Le Nôtre as well," silencing the ridicule on the spot.

Louis XIV bowed before nobody but his gardener. The two men shared a passion for nature, and I think that the king was proud of his château and very happy with his gardens. There was much satisfaction in being king of France, but few moments of true happiness. Le Nôtre, through his gardens, had offered the king a few of these happy moments. What was more, it was thanks to Le Nôtre that the king had his first great successes. A man of exemplary docility and great talent, Le Nôtre never refused the king—from the marshland of Versailles to the cesspool of Marly—meeting all of his challenges with satisfaction. The friendship between the men has already been commented upon by many authors, but it is true that, with so few written sources, everything must be left up to the imagination. Machiavellian, ambitious, manipulating—all of the darkest hypotheses about their relationship have been explored, but I prefer to see a common interest and two complementary personalities. Both were taciturn, both were visionaries; one authoritarian, the other obedient—it made for perfect chemistry.

Still, with age, and no doubt weary from a lifetime of submission, Le Nôtre began to rebel. Both men had grown old, but not old enough to slow the king's frenzy of projects. The king had a name to leave behind, whereas Le Nôtre was certain that his trees would outlive him—a mark of superiority of the gardener over his patron. The restless king entrusted the young Hardouin-Mansart with refurbishing the Bosquet des Sources, and the architect, more talented in sculpting stone than greenery, decided to raze the trees and replace them with a colonnade. Louis XIV, perhaps a bit ashamed, asked the opinion of his old friend, who clearly felt no need to hold his tongue. "Sire, what can I say? You turned a mason into a gardener and he has given you an example of his trade." The barb was unexpected, but Le Nôtre must have been hurt—childless, he saw his student and king betray his own work. Sometimes the sweetest trees bear bitter fruit.

Still, Louis XIV loved his gardener, appreciated his company, and showed his affection to the very end. Shortly before Le Nôtre's death at the age of eighty-seven, the thoughtful king, who was also beginning to feel the effects of age, had Le Nôtre accompany him in a sedan chair similar to his own in their promenades through the gardens. What higher honor was there for a subject than to be seated at the same level as his king? It is true that death would soon put them on equal footing, and perhaps Louis XIV was conscious of this. Nevertheless, what a beautiful parting image of two friends, the humble and the powerful, old men, sitting side by side among the renewed greenery of spring. To complete the picture, it should be added that Mansart followed the procession on foot. Claude Desgots, Le Nôtre's nephew, blithely unaware of the malice his uncle might have felt, described the scene as follows:

> *Le Nôtre, tears in his eyes at the thought of being seated beside the King, noticed Monsieur Mansart who was following them on foot and cried out "Sire, verily, my good father would not have believed his eyes had he seen me on a chair so near the greatest King on earth. It must be said that Your Majesty treats his mason and gardener very well."*

IF MANSART'S HEARING was decent, he probably winced at being referred to as a mason for a second time.

I must now confess, however, that I don't much like Le Nôtre. I admire his work, but I don't feel an affinity for the man. To cite Molière, an artist for whom, to the contrary, I feel a great deal of affinity, he was "from head to foot a man of mystery." Bug-eyed, his nose too large, both rough and haughty, he seems deeply sad. What is more, all of his work, for me, expresses sadness. His tamed trees feel submissive, lifeless, sterile, and cut in the image of the man, who though rich, lived in service and died childless. The detail that astonishes me the most is the words Louis XIV is said to have uttered to Le Nôtre: "You are a happy man." The words were more of an order than an observation. Having spoken little and written nothing, Le Nôtre is difficult to grasp, but when I consider his life and the portraits left behind by a few painters, I don't see a "happy man." To me he is a country mouse dressed up as a city mouse. When I contemplate the long, lifeless perspectives of his gardens and his austere peasant face dressed in noble garb, my heart grows cold with incomprehension. But the same is true for Louis XIV—it hardly astonishes me that they were friends! I can't pin down these seventeenth-century men. André Le Nôtre may have had a passion for gardens, but they weren't his calling. In the beginning he had wanted to become a painter, but he became a gardener for the worst reason in the world—because his father had been a gardener before him.

Besides, he was more architect than gardener. He designed the spaces, but he didn't cultivate them. The park of Versailles is above all a work of urban planning—perspectives, layouts on different levels, immense parterres, omnipresent statuary, and fountains. One must admit that the percentage of green is relatively restrained. The grounds were huge, dazzling, and sad—I think it's no coincidence that they were abandoned at the end of the reign of Louis XIV.

Although he popularized the style, Le Nôtre was not the true creator of the *jardin à la française*. Even at Versailles, he was inspired by the work of Claude Mollet and Jacques Boyceau de la Barauderie. The latter applied the recently discovered laws of optics to gardening. A "student" of Mansart, he transposed the two major theories of Baroque architecture—perspective and symmetry—into gardens. In his *Treatise of Gardening According to the Principles of Nature and Art*, Boyceau wrote, "Perspective shows the correct length of allées to those who wish to respect perfection. But often we want for them to be even longer so that they contain the entire space which is to be embellished, or so that they serve as a route that goes somewhere further."

Boyceau expresses the principle of symmetry in the following terms:

> *All the most beautiful things we can select will be defective and less agreeable if they are not positioned with symmetry and proper correspondence, for Nature also observes these laws in her perfect forms. Trees grow and spread their branches in equal proportions, their leaves are the same on each side, and their flowers divided into one or several parts with such reason that we cannot to hope to do better than attempt to follow this great example in this as in all of the other points which we have evoked.*

Le Nôtre, who worked with Boyceau at the Tuileries clearly made it a point of honor to fulfill this desire for symmetry and long perspectives. If one didn't know its date, one might think that Boyceau's text was written at Versailles, so much is the park a perfect example of its principles. Le Nôtre also borrowed details from Claude Mollet, also a gardener at the Tuileries. In his *Théâtre des plans et jardinages*, Mollet sets down his ideal garden—giving the proportions of the allées and indicating their importance to the overall plan, indicating that the parterres in *broderies* ought to be created from boxwood and contain flowers that bloom successively over the course of the year. Allées bordered by arbors, boxwood *broderies*, parallel and perpendicular axes, right angles cut off with slight recesses, allées that grow wider as they approach the château, the forms of the garden visible from the windows of the dwelling—the complete theory of the *jardin à la francaise* is already present. The classical garden taken to its apogee by Le Nôtre was nothing more than the logical result of Renaissance principles.

Far be it from me to minimize Le Nôtre's importance. Without him, the idea of the *jardin à la française* might not even exist. Thanks to Louis XIV, he had the immense merit of turning Boyceau and Mollet's ideas into reality, but he was not the originator of these ideas. He had good connections, means, and a king who adored him and whose reign lasted more than fifty years—but in spite of all that, I don't see the trace of genius. Le Nôtre was competent at magnifying the talent of his predecessors. What is more, there is little evolution in his work—over the course of his life he applied the same theories of Mollet and Boyceau. In general, I distrust notable figures when everybody seems to agree about them. The worst of these followers is probably Saint-Simon, who suspended his legendary acrimony when he spoke of Le Nôtre. "Le Notre had a probity an exactitude and an uprightness which made him esteemed and loved by everybody. He never forgot his position and was always perfectly disinterested. He worked for private people as for the King and with the same application seeking only to aid nature and to attain the beautiful by the shortest road. He was of a charming simplicity and truthfulness."[9]

I'm not one to read between the lines, but I see in these lines such condescension that each word almost seems like a slap in the face. In the end, Le Nôtre's greatest quality, in Saint-Simon's eyes, was his submissiveness. He "never stepped out of his place," he was a hard worker, but "selfless" and above all, naive—in a word, the perfect servant. Moreover, a few lines later, Saint-Simon opens his description of Le Nôtre's voyage to Italy by saying, "the Pope requested the King to loan him le Nôtre on these terms."

The king's gardener had been ennobled for a few years already, but he had the good taste to remain at his master's bidding. Saint-Simon's compliments are tinged with a disdain that I find repugnant, and I think Le Nôtre was partly responsible for them. If his servitude appalls me (it should be said that he rarely had a choice), I hate servility even more. At times, I imagine a Le Nôtre who was a schemer, servile and insincere, a courtier more than a gardener.

Was our glorious gardening ancestor an imposter? I don't think so, but I am sure that, although we owe him a great deal, we gardeners also owe him our image as servants. The cliché continues today—well-off families have their gardener and it is considered

---

9. Louis de Rouvroy Saint-Simon, *The Age of Magnificence: The Memoirs of the Duc de Saint-Simon*, de Gramon trans., Picadilly: Chatto and Windus, 1876, p. 169.

tasteful to leave the dirty work to him. Who fixes the car and takes out the trash? The "little gardener" who is always so "obliging" because one would prefer to pretend he is not simply "obliged." A slave and happy to be so, beloved and despised, such is the condition that we owe to Le Nôtre. During the same period, Nicolas Boileau wrote a poem, "Epistle to my gardener," which opens with the line, "Laborious valet of the most accommodating master."

Our fate is sealed. Gardeners, you will be lackeys! This is why, even though Le Nôtre is the "founding father" of our profession, his portrait would not hang in my personal gallery of ancestors. My "greats" number three: La Quintinie, Richard, and Briot.

To my eyes, Jean-Baptiste de La Quintinie, the founder of the King's Potager, was both a poet and scholar. Born in Charente in 1624, La Quintinie was not destined for a life in horticulture. After studying law, he received a post in Paris as a lawyer to the Court of Parliament and Master of the Queen's Petitions. Learned and well-read, La Quintinie was a great admirer of Pliny, wrote Latin poetry, and regularly peppered his writing with translations from Virgil and Horace.

In the preface to his estimable *Instruction pour les jardins fruitiers et potagers*, La Quintinie loosely translated and transposed Virgil's celebrated motto *O fortunatos nimium, sua si bona norint agricolas*[10] ("The usual condition of those who love agriculture is

---

10. Virgil, *The Georgics*, II, line 458.

happiness, as long as they know how to recognize it.") I never had the pleasure of studying Latin, but nothing is sweeter to my ears than the thousands of Latin names for plants. Scientific, they also contain countless lovely stories, simple and charming traces of a time when science still allowed itself to dream. The president of the Court of Auditors, Jean Tambonneau, entrusted his own son's education to La Quintinie. Rather than making his young disciple pore over the declensions of verbs, La Quintinie decided to take him to Italy to learn about art—on the principle that there is nothing like seeing and living to better learn and understand the world. This attitude toward education can only appeal to somebody like myself who was hardly an adept of schoolrooms. Better yet, the teacher learned alongside his student, particularly upon seeing the flamboyant gardens of Italy, the famous *giardini delle meraviglie* of which the gardens at the Villa d'Este are a magical example. I don't know what the young Tambonneau learned in their green and shady corners, but it was here that La Quintinie discovered his true passion. His law practice was finished. After that visit, he consecrated the rest of his life to the art of gardening. There is a detail I particularly like at the Villa d'Este: to return to the principal dwelling, the visitor has a choice between the path of Virtue, steep and rapid, or the path of Pleasure, whose slope is gentle and considerably longer. I don't know which path La Quintinie chose, but he had certainly found his way.

Tambonneau was a gracious prince. Although he had lost a tutor, he considered he had found a gardener and conferred the supervision of his greenhouses to La Quintinie. The former law-yer's talents were such that it was not long before he was stolen away by the great names of the period. He created the potagers (fruit and vegetable gardens) at Sceaux, Vaux-le-Vicomte, and Rambouillet, where he undoubtedly crossed paths with Le Nôtre. Why potagers? First, because the traditional function of the gar-den, of all gardens, even the Garden of Eden, was to nourish their inhabitants, and although the seventeenth century saw the appearance of purely ornamental gardens, it did not escape this rule. Besides—and this is my own personal interpretation—the potager provides something far more satisfying and sensual than the park. It calls upon one's senses—sight, hearing, smell, feel, and taste—as much as one's intelligence, and only with our senses can we appreciate a peach's perfume, a buzzing bee, the form of a vegetable, or the sweetness of a fruit. I was a gardener in the formal gardens long enough to know that one rapidly loses interest in trimming boxwood into perfect cones, but never in tasting the strawberries that one has raised. To me, there is nothing astonish-ing in the fact that the cold Le Nôtre did his best to complicate the design of his borders and parterres while La Quintinie was picking ever more delicate and luscious pears.

Both men were part of Nicolas Fouquet's team at Vaux, and they would work together again at Versailles. La Quintinie was given the direction of the former potager of Louis XIII. A far more modest man than Le Nôtre (it is said that he hated to appear in public), he was just as successful as his better-known colleague and was richly compensated for his work; in 1670, the post of director of the fruit and vegetable gardens for the royal household was created specifically for him. Le Nôtre and La Quintinie had been granted different but equivalent positions: Louis XIV was faithful to the eternal practice of "dividing to conquer." This two-headed empire did not last long. It became necessary to enlarge the potager as the number of courtiers flocking to Versailles increased, and La Quintinie, to the delight of Le Nôtre, was relegated to the banks of the "stinking pond" that would later become the Pièce d'Eau des Suisses. La Quintinie would have preferred the domain of Clagny and continually lamented the ground that was left to him by Le Nôtre, but his complaints fell on deaf ears.

The project was slow, laborious, and expensive. Between 1678 and 1683 the plot was worked with spade and pickax to render it cultivable, at the extravagant cost of a million livres. To dry the swamp, the ground was laid with a series of drains that were covered with the earth from the excavation of the Pièce d'Eau des Suisses. But this unproductive soil had to be improved, and better earth from the hills of Satory was brought to the site with a complex system of machinery. Once this challenge was overcome, the potager started to take shape, according to the plans of La Quintinie and thanks to the masonry of Mansart. Today's potager is very similar to that of La Qunintinie's day. It extends over approximately twenty-five acres. A large square, it is divided into sixteen smaller squares of vegetables, surrounded by low-trained fruit tree espaliers, and in its center, there is a large circular basin. A terrace was created so that the king could admire and show off his crops without having to literally descend to their level. Nestled behind the high walls that surround the large square-shaped plot are twenty-nine walled gardens protecting a treasure of fruit trees, rare vegetables, and delicate smaller fruits, with the walls and terraces allowing for a variety of microclimates and exposures to sunlight. La Quintinie was a genius of gardening. His combination of scientific rigor, inventiveness, and passion for his craft allowed him to pull off incredible feats. If Manet's painting of a spear of asparagus revolutionized Impressionist painting, La Quintinie had shaken the world of horticulture with his asparagus long before. As most people know, *Asparagus officinalis* thrusts its shoots from the earth in the spring. In the seventeenth century, however, seasons were more than just a nebulous concept of the fashion industry, and in a good year, one could only eat asparagus two months out of the year (at court, anyway). That which is rare is also expensive, and at that period, sought after. Moreover, Louis XIV adored asparagus, leading La Quintinie to have the brilliant idea of growing asparagus in primitive cold frames. Panes of glass captured the sun's rays, warming a layer of straw spread beneath the plants, allowing the king to propose the precious vegetable at his table year-round; the *primeur,* or greengrocer, offering precious fruits and vegetables out of season thus was born. Paradoxically, La Quintinie was a discreet man who disliked society salons and rarely came to the royal table to savor his accomplishments, unlike Le Nôtre, who I think must have been as green with jealousy as the celebrated and savory productions of his gardening colleague.

With the encouragement of Louis XIV, La Quintinie pursued his experiments to improve the appearance, taste, and production of the royal fruits and vegetables. He tried different methods of pruning and treatment. Near the king's gate, he created a "garden on the bias," building screens oriented along a north-south axis against which he advanced the peach harvest, thanks to maximum exposure to the sun. In those days, France was not a land of desserts; meals, even feasts, ended with fruit— giving it special importance. Louis XIV adored figs, and yet growing figs at Versailles amounted to no less than a miracle. La Quintinie pulled it off by growing them in large pots, for he had noticed that it was the cold that most often killed the fig trees. The pots allowed the figs to be taken inside for the winter, like the orange trees, and then brought out at the best moment in the spring. He created, according to the principles of the Orangerie, a "figuerie"—a slightly lower parcel of land abutting a large building that protected the spot from the weather. Figs were also trained against walls. A few years later, more than seven hundred trees were producing multiple varieties of figs: Grosse-Jaune, Grosse-Blanche, Grosse-Violette, Verte, and Angélique. Louis XIV could enjoy his favorite fruit as early as mid-June.

I admire the botanist's skill, his passion for his work. Concerned about passing on his knowledge, La Quintinie left us his

*Instruction pour les jardins fruitiers et potagers*, a treatise that is still used today and is, to my eyes, like poetry, or at least a declaration of love. Here is how La Quintinie speaks of his darling figs:

> *A good fig is the fruit among all others which deserves*
> *the best place in espalier (in warm countries, it would be*
> *inconvenienced by such treatment), and by consequence,*
> *the esteem to which it is due: one only has to observe the*
> *movement of the shoulders and eyebrows of those who*
> *taste it and the quantity that can be consumed without any*
> *danger to one's health.* [11]

These lines are filled with such tender gentleness! I read in them the pride and almost filial love of the creator of these succulent little creatures. I don't know whether La Quintinie was a poet, but I know that he knew how to observe, pick, and ripen both fruits and images. All of La Quintinie's treatise is a model of kindness and accuracy. He has taught me not only to know my craft, but also to love it. I don't have much esteem for Louis XIV, but to think of him yielding to the forbidden fruit and reveling in his figs, an eyebrow slightly lifted, and his neck retracting between his shoulders in a gesture of prudish pleasure, is to finally catch a glimpse of the man behind the glacial sovereign.

---

11. *Instruction pour les jardins fruitiers et potagers*, Arles: Actes Sud, 1999, p. 432.

The botanist's careful and loving descriptions remind me of those written by a more recent author, Francis Ponge. The poet also evokes the childish delectation of tasting a fig, held whole in the mouth before biting into the flesh and letting it melt, like candy. A versatile fruit, Ponge's fig is both "a storeroom of annoyances for the teeth" and a "pacifier" that "by chance, becomes entirely edible." Invariably, it yields the "glimmering altar of its interior" and the miracle of its "purple pulp, gratified with seeds." The enamored poet turned this unlikely muse into the emblem of his art: "Such is the elasticity (of the spirit) of words and of poetry as I consider it."[12]

I don't have any poetic pretensions, and quite honestly, I don't think that I have poetry between my teeth every time I bite into a fig. Still, I find in Ponge's simple, precise, and almost unnervingly accurate words the same delicacy that I feel belonged to my master gardener, La Quintinie.

But let's leave the figs for now. La Quintinie reserved corners of his potager for growing other produce, describing them with the evocative French words of *melonnière* and *prunelaye*. As befitted a learned man, La Quintinie composed more than a few lines of Latin, but it is in reading the long lists of fruits and vegetables that he recommended for the king's table that I find the poetry he put into this work. This classical gardener

---

12. Francis Ponge, *Pièces*, Paris: Poésie Gallimard, 1971, p. 179. Translated by Christopher Brent Murray

produced fruits with names that were each more delicious than the last: Bon-Chrétien d'hiver pears, which were offered to the Siamese ambassadors and the doge of Venice, and varieties with consonances that are so French that they sound, to my ears, better than any of Corneille's long tirades: Cousinotte, Nivette, Rousseline, Orgeran, Nasturces, Pomme d'Etoile, Jérusalem, Francatu, Haute-Bonté, Blandilalie, Rouvezeau, and Petit-Bon.

Almost nothing is known of the relationship between Le Nôtre and La Quintinie, apart from the fact that the botanist regularly complained of the land left to him by the king's favorite. I think it would be hard to imagine two men who were less similar. The Greeks had Apollo and Dionysus, the intellectuals Voltaire and Rousseau, and the fans of the sixties had the Beatles and the Stones (with Sartre and Raymond Aron as a bonus). We gardeners have La Quintinie and Le Nôtre, a botanist and an architect, a scholar and a man who left nothing more in writing than his signature at the bottom of a plan, a homebody and a socialite—even the genders of the articles that form their names are opposed! To me, they are two fathers, one spiritual, the other biological. The heritage of one weighs on my shoulders and often exasperates me, without pushing me so far as to deny his important influence; the other is the ancestor I would choose, the man I would like to resemble, but whose model still seems, today, inaccessible. Le Nôtre dreamed of becoming a painter and, failing that, became a gardener. La Quintinie could have risen to the highest spheres of social recognition but chose to make himself a gardener. Therein lies the difference between an artist and a good artisan. Le Nôtre couldn't do anything else, but La Quintinie didn't want to do anything else—in his hands, gardening rediscovered its nobility and through his book, a veritable poetic art. Le Nôtre wrote nothing and died childless, without any veritable students. Twenty years later, his gardens followed him into oblivion. The *jardin à la française* was replaced by the *jardin à l'anglaise*. In horticultural history, Le Nôtre's aesthetic is among the most renowned, but it also lasted for the shortest time. Perhaps this is because, in the end, he didn't have that much to pass down. After all, if one wanted to re-create the gardens of Versailles, it would suffice to read the works of Claude Mollet. Le Nôtre left us a name and a condition. La Quintinie left us a book—in my eyes, the best sort of legacy there is.

To round out this portrait gallery, I'd like to mention two names, those of Claude Richard and Jacques Briot. Richard was also a genius botanist. In the service of Louis XV, he has remained celebrated in the small world of gardeners for a touching story about his creation of a new sort of flower, the white double aster known as the Reine-Marguerite. Louis XV was proud of his botanist but didn't believe this kind of invention would be possible. Richard worked tirelessly, improving the variety and developing a more efficient system of greenhouses heated by ducts. Finally, he invited the king to come view his work. Louis XV dubiously stepped into the greenhouses only to find himself in front of a perfumed bed of flowers in which *to my beloved King* had been "written" using the triumphant Reine-Marguerites—a prime example of sycophancy and a forerunner of ad campaigns encouraging us to "say it with flowers."

But it's not for this episode that I have affection for Claude Richard—his floral inscriptions are, for me, nothing more than an exercise in style, an ancestor to municipal gardens in which a floral "Welcome to Petuniaville" stands out from a lawn that has been cut too short, and which would make any true garden enthusiast head for the hills. Claude Richard was already a renowned botanist before coming to Versailles. On numerous occasions he had been solicited by courtiers. He finally agreed to put his talents to work in the service of Louis XV on the condition that he receive his orders only from the king himself. Richard had his way, and was paid directly from His Majesty's personal budget. As somebody who has to suffer repeated, protracted meetings, and mountains of paperwork, I can only admire the visionary lucidity of my talented predecessor!

Jacques Briot was the head gardener at the Trianon. Fascinated with agricultural botany, he created a new variety of tree in 1858, *Aesculus carnea briotii*, the flamboyant red-flowered horse chestnut. Sadly, many of them have been removed and replaced with the ordinary, white-flowered variety. I have nothing against these trees, apart from finding them rather commonplace, but I think it is unfortunate to see them populating the garden of Versailles to the detriment of their red-flowered cousins. What would be more natural than to replant the tree in its natural setting and to see it prosper in the ground that once gave it life? In a more general manner, I always try to conserve and even to return to a certain integrity in the park at Versailles—in this sense, my job is radically counter that of my forebears: where Briot and Richard created new varieties of plants, I push myself to find the matricaria, dame's rocket, and rose campion that once flowered along the paths strolled by Marie Antoinette.

WHAT MAKES A good gardener? The essential ingredient can be reduced to a single word: joy. Our work may be tiring, but it is also extremely gratifying. First of all, and not least of all, our surroundings are beautiful. While the modern man leaves his car or commuter train to work in the cramped quarters often misleadingly called "open space," we spend our days in the fresh air, among flowers and trees. In what other profession does the lunch break take place in a garden? I think of my happy lunches each time I see an unfortunate man or woman who has escaped from the cafeteria to enjoy a sandwich (perhaps even a bad one) on one of the first sunny days in April. Gardens are calming. It is revealing to see how fast people walk down the street on Paris's Rue de Rivoli, and then slow down and take their time as soon as they set foot in the Tuilieries's gardens. This is a sign of a garden's marvelous capacity to give us, if not happiness, then at least rest.

Although it was not often the case in the past, for many of my gardeners, the profession brought them social recognition. Up until the 1980s, gardeners were often from humble backgrounds and mostly came from the country. Not knowing what to do, these half-consenting victims of France's rural exodus came to Versailles to take up the work their fathers had taught them: working the land. They all remained faithful to the gardens for having saved them from a city life. Instead of wasting away in a factory, they made the gardens grow and prosper, and received daily compliments from admiring visitors.

Work in the gardens is a collective effort, sometimes with music in the background, and always with the possibility for good conversation; our craft is not one practiced in silence. But should one need to be left in peace, it is enough to go to the depths of the park or even to just lower one's head and fall out of the dialogue. The seasons give rhythm to our work—not trade shows, the back-to-school routine, or traditional summer vacations, but spring, summer, autumn, and winter—masters that, believe me, are far more gentle and significant. In June, it is the length of the daylight that keeps us at work, not some pile of overdue paperwork. In December, it is the pleasure of returning to one's well-heated house after a day spent outside in the cold. We savor the rain because it spares us the need to water, and we wait in anxiety for the first frosts and snows. There is a certain sweetness in knowing that one is beholden to the climate—a higher force that is regular, at times inopportune, but never stressed-out or hysterical. In contact with nature, we know we must take care of it: pruning, weeding, planting—our work breathes. In a society filled with lifeless materials, it is particularly beneficial to know one is caring for the living. Our plants and flowerbeds are like people! This is how one knows a bad gardener. He acts without taking into account a plant's identity—he cuts everything according to the same rule, following books instead of listening to nature. He can identify a hawthorn, has records, and is aware of any number of details, but he doesn't know the old hawthorn on the little wall behind the spring. Perhaps I'm biased, but in the end, it is far more agreeable to pick a tomato when it is fully ripe, a tomato you have grown yourself, than it is to give a PowerPoint presentation in front of a dozen executives in suits and ties. This is another important detail—we are free to dress as we please. No matter what happens, we can smoke, talk, or be silent whenever we like. The garden is a place of freedom for visitors just as it is for those who take care of it. One has to believe that the gardener is happier for it.

# DEAD LEAVES
≈≈≈≈≈≈≈≈≈≈≈≈≈

I DON'T MEAN any disrespect to Jacques Prévert, but dead leaves are not collected using a shovel as the lyric of his famous song "Les feuilles mortes" claims. In the old days, gardeners used rakes, as was the case when I arrived at Versailles. Today, leaf blowers appear everywhere at the beginning of autumn. In almost forty years at Versailles, I have been witness to a veritable technological revolution. This is all the more unusual given that the gardener's trade is one of the few to have not evolved in the popular imagination. The gardener continues to be represented in his straw hat, rubber boots, blue apron, and bushy moustache, and I continue to be amused by the astonished surprise of people who see me for the first time "in plain clothes," dressed the same as everybody else. Our supposed uniform is an integral part of our image.

This use of technology is a recent evolution, particularly at Versailles, a place more inclined to archaisms. When I began working in the château's gardens in 1976, the park still looked as it did in the 1950s, just older. Visually speaking, the trees were those of the postwar period. The fact that it takes fifty years for a tree to reach maturity has an impact on gardening trends; they move at a less frenetic pace. Besides, in this insular, often retrograde world, people's mentalities also resist change. I was very young in those days and I still remember the old-fashioned atmosphere that reigned over the gardens. I had entered, not without a certain pleasure, a timeless, unchanged world of the traditionalist—clichéd images right out of the old black-and-white photography that then occupied a major part of my free time. The old gardeners still talked about the veterans of the First World War who had been hired at the end of the conflict. Many of them had been injured and were employed as guards, leaving them a solid reputation as being good-for-nothing. The idea that, "If you don't really want to work, you can always become a guard," still made my colleagues chuckle. I also remember a cowherd who still wore wooden clogs—of course, he was Dutch, but to me, he represented the *passéiste* attitude that reigned at Versailles. In covering the distance between Parly and the château there was a difference of fifty years—making the Versailles of 1976 a veritable time machine.

The grand ceremony began in autumn. As the lawns of the park slowly became covered in leaves, the gardeners worked their large rakes toothless clearing the allées. It was a long, slow, and seemingly interminable chore. Every day new leaves fell, undoing the previous day's labor. Patient and docile, we set to work anew, making the park both accessible and impeccable before the arrival of the first visitors. I still remember those bitter, damp mornings, too gloomy for the sun to warm our hands.

The dry leaves, almost weightless, crackling beneath our feet, filled the air with a tenacious odor that was at once acrid and cold, contrasting with the warmth of their color. Orange, brown, and bronze, the park became grandiose, bringing me to understand how autumn is the subtlest season. Paradoxically, there was nothing monotonous about the work—it was like a dance. We repeated the gestures, always the same, always with the fear that we might not reach the end of our work. The meager gardeners' quadrille knew itself to be outmatched by its dance partner. A single gust of wind could erase the morning's work. This ballet of rakes and leaves waltzed away the time from September to December. We had to be more persistent than nature herself. One day, she would miraculously surrender, relenting and admitting defeat. We would load our wheelbarrows and wagons to take our captives to the depths of the park, where they formed ephemeral mountains that gradually broke down to create the following year's compost.

Nearby, the spectacle had already been replaced by others. No doubt it was as much out of tradition as for the beauty of the gesture that we continued this way at Versailles—it was a rare and gracious time, and for me, that was justification enough.

Pruning season was similarly special. The park was old and the trees had grown particularly tall. Every year, the gardeners were transformed into giants, mounted on perilous stilts and wielding enormous billhooks to reach the treetops. To the end of the horizon along Versailles's interminable allées, they waged a strange, even comical war: giant gardeners against titanic trees. The struggle was fierce—there were numerous falls. I was only working in the flowerbeds, but I looked on in amusement, with a twinge of jealousy, to see my swaggering colleagues, with their tattooed biceps and cigarettes, become timid and clumsy atop their ten-foot wooden perches. Extraordinarily, and in spite of regrettable incidents with pruning shears, errors, accidents, and interminable evening up of proportions, the final result was always impeccable. Today we use an extremely complicated piece of equipment, respect every law of geometry to the letter, but for some reason, to the eye, the lines seem far less straight than they used to.

One of Versailles's most beautiful archaisms (without any irony intended) was the use of horses. I arrived too late to see the horses "working" in the park, but in sifting through the archives to learn how work techniques in the gardens had evolved, I discovered their former presence. The last horses in Paris were still working in the years just after the Second World War, but even in those days, they had become an exception. In Versailles, there was no need to go back to the war—in January 1967, the veterinarian Henri Debrosse announced with great ceremony the death "of the horse Gracieux, from the château of Versailles," afflicted with generalized paralysis. The declaration, written in turquoise ink, was pinned to two carbon copies of a letter written by the head gardener of Versailles to the caretaker of the domain of Versailles and the Trianon. After the banal "I have the honor of bringing you the news that the gardens' workhorse died this afternoon," my predecessor continued in a tone that seems rather comical and provocative, given the circumstances: "I think it would be good to replace the horse rather quickly, as a horse is indispensable in the nursery. If possible, it would be preferably a rather strong horse, because most of the work done by the horse is physical labor."

And the curator's response? "I don't intend to request the horse's replacement as the motorized equipment now in our possession ensures the proper function of the gardens. However, for moving the orange trees at the beginning and end of the summer season, we will have to find, and without too much delay, either a supplementary tractor or a horse." A horse's labor was still deemed necessary—a mere year before the social upheavals of 1968 and our modern age.

The curator seems to have been in favor of progress: Gracieux was probably replaced by a tractor. Technology has certainly accomplished miracles, and far be it from me to play the crank or fall victim to the retrograde "Versailles Syndrome," but I regret the abandonment of horses. Tractors allow us to work more quickly, but they are noisy and polluting. The tractor's strength can also be a problem. It compacts the earth and damages the roots of certain trees, and in the end, creates a sort of nuisance. In an ornamental and historic garden, we ought to be more bound to aesthetics than to productivity. Certainly, this is a luxury in our day, but there is no need for us to work faster. What point is there in using these huge, heavy, dirty, and expensive machines better suited to factory farms? Sometimes I even wonder whether the preference for machines isn't just another form of snobbery, or the childish passion for gadgets that possesses the enthusiasts of electronic devices and SUVs. At Versailles, it is felt that we need the best, the newest, and the most expensive, even if the results turn out to be disastrous. Unlike tractors, a horse doesn't pollute, destroys nothing, and makes work more agreeable for its gardener companion, and even for the visitors watching the regular garden work, which becomes a sort of spectacle. Bringing flowers from the nursery to the planting site on a horse-drawn cart instead of with a truck and trailer might take a few minutes longer, but it would be beautiful. What visitor wouldn't be charmed by the sight of a horse outside the palace windows? We might lose a little time, but in doing so, we'd add to the dream of Versailles. I proposed to my superiors that trash could be collected with horse-drawn carts instead of the hideous little garbage trucks with their flashing lights that we currently use, slow and stinking vehicles that ruin our visitors' walks. I'm persuaded that tourists would be less negligent about leaving behind their litter if they saw the horse at work. Of course, my request wasn't taken seriously.

Modern machinery is efficient, but sad, cold, and without any pleasure. With the horse, there was a contact, warmth, and complicity that transformed the most laborious of jobs into a pleasure. There is something good and gentle in returning to the stable in the evening, exhausted, in the company of one's horse, picking up the pace because the horse can "smell home." You keep one another company. And it's far more agreeable to bandage an animal than to replace a broken part. When the animal grows tired, you take notice, there is emotion. You are anxious for his health to improve, perhaps because he is so linked to your work, but also out of affection. You are happy to see him at the beginning of the day, and to know that he is going to be your work partner. In the winter, when trucks refuse to start, the only emotion one feels is that of exasperation.

Versailles was once full of animals. In the archives, I came across a note to a gardener named Monsieur Buffé, dating from 1957. "I have noticed, for a while now, a certain number of chickens strolling around Châteauneuf without knowing to whom they belong. It would be preferable that the owners of these chickens keep them inside their coops, and that they not be allowed to stray outside or in other areas not reserved for them."

It touches me to imagine this brood of poultry, clucking and proud, "strolling" among the American tourists. The notes I receive most often concern forgotten packaging and detritus... how I wish they were about stray chickens! And I'm not the only one; it is often said that Malraux, in the days when he lived in the Pavillon de Lanterne, expressly requested that his chauffeur take care to avoid what were probably the same chickens—and that the minister even had him stop the car so he could watch the "eccentric" parade pass, to borrow his own word.

And now? The park echoes with the noise of tractors and rototillers. Plastic and motors have become our masters, and the gardens vroom and rumble like an electric power plant—the poetry of the place has fled in the face of so much ugliness. The graceful world of yesterday's tools has perished, sacrificed upon the altar of technology. I was happy when I knew how to prune a tree, but there was no joy in learning to use a leaf blower. Pulled along inside the cabin of the tractor, the gardener now knows the comfort of those who work seated but he has been stripped of his authenticity. From the morning onward, the park is invaded by colossal chain saws and gigantic lawn mowers. The latter have grown so large and expensive that one of our latest acquisitions cost nearly a hundred thousand euros. The gardener is kept prisoner in a large, air-conditioned cabin from which he can barely see what he is doing. It is no longer the gardener who mows, but two immense blades that cut a swath twice as wide as the machine "he pilots," cut off from the world. His work is not mowing, but machine operation. What soul and grace are to be found in such factory work? The lawns are more perfectly square and geometric than the eye can perceive; not the slightest blade of grass is longer than another, a perfection that saddens the imagination and distresses the soul. What interest is there in shaving off every irregular detail, in cutting the buttercup and daisy that stood out from the grass and rendered it more beautiful? Our work is to give order to nature, not to participate in a massacre. With the old mowers, the gardener could see what he was doing, which allowed him to mow around things, to avoid objects and let pass charming differences such as the lawn's wildflowers.

Chain saws roar and cut down trees with a facility that I think dangerous. Of course, they allowed us to clean up the park after the storm more quickly, and as a result, open it to the public much earlier, but the chain saw has also brought about a number of irremediable losses. When it took three days to cut down an oak, when the work was slow and difficult, one could be sure that trees had been removed for a good reason. Now, gardeners are more likely to act upon a whim—cutting down trees at will, without much reflection—and too bad if the neighboring tree gets taken out as well. The work is not done as well—it's butchery, but it doesn't matter, because it is done quickly.

Versailles has become a construction site where the tourist is a nuisance. Many used to ask for photos with the gardeners—we were part of the landscape. The pose in front of the Grand Canal with the gardener in his muddy apron, rake in hand, was a classic. But who would want their picture taken with a weirdo running a machine that looks like a gigantic vacuum cleaner, whose face is barely visible from beneath his helmet, the whole combination in a giant, noisy cloud of dust stinking of exhaust fumes? The worst part is that the manufacturers of this equipment probably pride themselves on having turned the "vulgar gardener" into a veritable outdoor technician.

It's the smell and the noise that bother me the most. Imagine the delicate, invigorating scent of freshly cut grass masked by waves of diesel; horses' warm breath supplanted by rumbling engines. In the old days there were as many sounds in the garden as there were different sorts of tools, and the concert of Versailles's implements was like that of a village band. It may not have been a masterpiece, of course, but it was pleasant. Now the noise is so loud and unbearable that most of my men work with hearing protection. Everything that was once alive is now mechanical. Technology certainly brought a new ease and accuracy, but apart from these ultimately less important details, the new equipment has caused our quality of life to deteriorate. Technical progress in my profession has allowed for improved comfort, but not improved living, and it would be a serious error to confuse the two. You aren't happier in a leather armchair; you're just better seated.

And it all goes to waste! We once used the fallen leaves we gathered as compost, with the end of one season assuring the fertility of the next. Today, the strident, fuel-hungry blowers chase the leaves to the low-lying edges of the park where they are burned on a pyre lit with the aid of additional gasoline. Not only have the leaves become useless, they pollute. They are collected more quickly, but a new chore has been grafted upon the old one—what good is it to save time if we only go on to lose it in useless work?

The same is true for the wood. Instead of being used as firewood for heating, no sooner are the logs cut than they are burned—useful to nobody. The most shocking example came in the days following the big storm. During a period when thousands of trees had been cut down, the price of wood didn't change by a cent! It is even forbidden for outsiders to collect fallen branches in the park. Wood has the misfortune of being considered a waste product, in the same category as garbage—it is carted off to the incinerator, which, of course, functions on oil.

Although it is praiseworthy to want to spare human labor, I fear that the motivations of many are rarely very altruistic. All that has changed is that we consume Saudi fuel instead of our own, and I doubt that the exchange has been profitable. In any case, it was unnecessary in my line of work. Moreover, the damage done to the environment is far from negligible. Tractors compact and damage the earth. The fact that a factory producing cars is a source of pollution surprises nobody, but the idea that we gardeners are also damaging nature is another thing altogether! Doesn't it seem aberrant that those entrusted with making the ground flourish and prosper poison it instead? In recent decades, and in spite of my efforts to the contrary, the volume of pesticide and herbicide used at Versailles has doubled. I am struck dumb when I read the yearly report on toxic products that have been used on-site—an activity that is not only harmful to the earth but worse, also to some of our employees. Of course, there is no end to the safety warnings, but the means to put them into action are far less abundant. Not long ago, my staff received a carefully prepared lecture on the latest toxic products (the more deadly they become, the less often the word *poison* is used—French is a language of euphemisms). After their magnificent class in the art and manner of using poison, as well as its proper storage in special "total security" storage units, their shipment of products arrived without a hitch—but the storage units did not. It's far too easy to go about one's work in good conscience when, often, the worst damage has already been done. Over about forty years (the blink of an eye as far as nature is concerned), I have noticed a serious deterioration in the wildlife around Versailles. Beyond the visual and sound pollution of the tractors and security cars, the soil quality and level of the water table have become worrisome. It didn't take a century of herbicide and the famous dichlorodiphenyltrichloroethane, or DDT, to damage beyond recovery the quality of certain terrains, the populations of certain animals, and doubtless, the health of certain individuals. When I think that it used to be customary for gardeners to taste their spray to verify the concentration! Without wanting to play the "bird of ill omen," I must say that today's gardens are under threat.

In my first years at Versailles, I heard turtledoves and cuckoos when I woke up in the morning. Now I only hear cars passing on the nearby highway, and, since the storm, I can see the Parly II shopping mall. Things were very different not that long ago.

It has to be said that the technological revolution that the rest of France saw in the 1950s and 1960s didn't really arrive in Versailles until the 1980s. In a strange way, it was as though the technology followed, even pursued, me. The first instant soups and washing machines meant to liberate the housewife appeared in my childhood; modern record players showed up when I was a teenager; and when I began working at Versailles, traditional tools began to be replaced by electric ones. Looking back, it almost seems like I brought the miracle of electricity in my wake when I rode down the slope from Celle-Saint-Cloud to Versailles on my motorized bike.

The revolution was all the more drastic because it saw the modification and even disappearance of objects that had existed for thousands of years. The dibble, for example, had been around since the Paleolithic age. Of course, it hasn't been made from mammoth tusk for quite some time, but I guarantee that there are far fewer differences between the prehistoric dibbles and those of my first years at Versailles than there are between those modern dibbles and the machines we use today. Agricultural tools took form, if not definitively, very early: the ancient Greeks were already using hoes, fruit-harvesting hooks, rakes, spades, and shovels. The objects evolved very little over the course of time. The T- or Y-shape of the spade's handle, for example, a form that allows for a better grip, was developed in ancient Rome. Until the industrial revolution, the blacksmith continued to work with techniques that were ancestral in the true meaning of the word; his methods had been the same for centuries. Tools were precious, rare, and individual, created specifically to fit the shape and strength of the gardener's hand. Often the gardener would decorate his tools by engraving a flower and leaves or a motto, sometimes his monogram. It wasn't unusual to have the tool blessed along with the animals of his farm. In a sense, the tool was made-to-measure—if nobody could adapt to it after the gardener's death, it was melted down and reforged, because iron was rare.

There is nothing banal in the fact that the tool was, in its very conception, an extension of a person, so much so, that when you received one, you received the weight of the centuries. The tool had passed down from generation to generation and articulated the gardener's heritage—taking on a tool was to adopt the mark of one's predecessor and all those before him, to hold it all in one's hand. The tool transmitted a symbolic handshake, which is probably the source of its emotional weight—when you took the scythe in hand and accomplished a movement that cut the grass, you echoed a gesture that had been made for millenia. The presence of the past in such a simple movement was loaded but reassuring—one was participating in an activity as old as humanity itself. What a pleasure to be dubbed a human being! Such is no longer the case. It took a long time for the rapport between man and tool to shift—modernity has been steadily chipping away at it since the nineteenth century, but the final shift only took place in the 1960s or 1970s. Versailles knows something about what it means to break with a slow, centuries-old evolution, a break that makes it so that things will never be the same again—this is the true meaning of a revolution.

In my house I have a reproduction of Caillebotte's *Les Jardiniers*, a work of art I particularly admire. The painting shows the universe I discovered upon my arrival in Versailles, and yet it dates to 1875! Nothing had changed over the course of a century. One sees a potager, bordered by flowerbeds and fruit trees pruned in espalier against a tall cypress hedge. Along a wall, portable cold frames protect tender young plants, and in the foreground, a gardener waters his lettuce. Sleeves rolled up, blue apron, and straw hat, he has the serious attitude of one who loves his work—entirely focused on the task at hand. He takes it so seriously that nothing can distract him, not even his colleague advancing towards him with two more watering cans that seem to be full. The men work barefoot—apart from wooden clogs, few shoes resist water, mud, and snow. In 1976, the gardeners' feet were shod, but some of them, particularly the old-timers, would have have preferred to work barefoot. Caillebotte took care to hide the faces of the men—beneath the shadow of their hats— and to dress all of them the same way for they are the essence of *jardiniers*, the archetype that many of us still see straying in the corners of our memory. In my case, the image takes on a particular significance: Caillebotte's gardeners are the men who welcomed me to Versailles.

Behind them, a line of glass cloches rests upon the ground. Cloches were used both as shelter and a source of warmth for plants, and most often used to grow melons. Each young plant had its own little "hat," which I would lift in the morning with curiosity and concern, to see how the plant was growing. A tiny clay pot also had to be slipped under the edge of the cloche, to allow the air to circulate. They were pretty little pots—nothing rare, of course, but it was still sad to break one. Soon they were made of green plastic: disposable, supposedly unbreakable, and hideous. What was it all for? Terra-cotta pots were fragile and inconvenient, but we took care of them—and some people would even take the leftover "survivors" to reuse when we received a new shipment. Even the most insignificant of objects had a heavy, prestigious quality that made them seem worthy of admiration. Perhaps it's just the passage of time that makes me think so—but I guarantee that most plastic pots wind up in the garbage long before they become useless. Who would decorate their living room or store their pens in a plastic flowerpot? To save a trace of all of these charming, outdated objects, I, along with a few friends and craftsmen, have decided to start reproducing a few tools the old way—perhaps the only battle from which a clay flowerpot can emerge victorious.

It may be abundance that has made us so negligent. It is much easier, these days, to buy new tools, and we never run short of anything, especially plastic. The most glaring difference is that we no longer repair anything. What does it matter if a gardener breaks his rake when we have three hundred others hanging in the storage shed? Before, for simple economic reasons, tools were repaired—because they had to last. They were also more solid. At Versailles, the gardeners were responsible for their tools— they owned them and had to pay for damages. Upon his arrival, a young gardener received a spade and a watering can, and he was expected to keep them for the length of his career—it was better to repair than replace. A tool was the gardener's first companion and witness—it was with the tool and thanks to the tool that one could do one's job, if it was taken care of, oiled, and cleaned. And if a tool happened to get lost, one searched until it was found. Soon, the tool became irreplaceable, because it contained memories of one's own life. And when you have spent hours improving, mastering, and patching a tool, you hold it all the more dear.

I remember breaking the handle of my spade. I waited anxiously for a new handle to be attached. When I saw my spade restored to life in the hands of the repairman, I swore I would be far more careful in the future. I was happy. Today, spades have fiberglass handles, which are handy because they don't break—but they mark the end of the tools' miraculous renewal. Already precious for economic reasons, the tool over time increased in value for sentimental reasons. You were proud to pass it down, and when you received a tool from an older colleague, you were touched: you knew you were holding his entire life in your hands. I knew gardeners who asked to bring their tools with them when they retired so that they could pass them down to their grandsons, also requesting one last new apron for their Sundays. These were never used, but kept, carefully folded in mothballs as a trophy from a past life. It also pains me to think of the gardeners a few years older than me, who truly knew the old days, who leave the profession. What will they have to pass down to us—artificial flowers in a plastic pot?

Gardening equipment has become sad. It is merely functional, austere, and depressingly ugly. I remember the seed packets of my childhood. They were decorated with exuberant and imaginary flowers and fruits—veritable magic beans—with bright colors and curving vegetation rising up to the rosy-cheeked face of a gardener, round and muscular like a circus strong man, the very picture of abundance. The drawings had another purpose, for many gardeners couldn't read. The images—like the stained glass windows in churches that once were used to tell the stories of the Bible—told them the destiny of the seeds contained within. Today seeds, like airplane peanuts, are sold in vacuum-sealed packages in sober, pictureless foil envelopes, where one reads, in poorly printed and hapazardly placed text, the name of the plant and an expiration date. Gray and always colder than your hand, they feel almost funereal. The plant hasn't even begun to grow and its death already seems imminent. Personally, it doesn't make me feel like planting the seeds.

Certain tools have all but disappeared. The large, majestic willow baskets, whose lightness always surprised me, were replaced by garbage bags, identical and ugly, which my crew wastes without batting an eye. How can I hold it against them? Who would give a fig for a plastic bag? Plastic is the enemy.

The same is the case for watering cans. They used to come in a thousand different shapes—little ones with little roses for small pots, huge cans for large surfaces, long spouts and tiny roses for the rare flowers in the greenhouses, long spouts and large roses to reach into the middle of broad flowerbeds (also known as the Raveneau model). With fixed or removable roses, in copper, iron, wood, steel, or an alloy, each one corresponded to an individual situation. They had something about them, and something about the individuality of their forms and their clumsy soldering made one think of the war wounded. There was childish pleasure in picking out a watering can. In the shadowy depths of a garden shed, like Ali Baba's cavern, you might hesitate between thirty different sorts, searching through the dust until you found just the right one. Now, kept prisoner in the back of the garden truck, sit fifty prefabricated watering cans—at most four different sizes and two different shapes, all the same depressing hue of dark green. Even this limited variety is no longer interesting. It used to be amusing, even a little magical, to uncover odd tools and use them to water the parterres. Today, the watering cans used by my crews are the same as those found in any ordinary suburban garden. The professional's tools are now accessible to everybody. The only sign distinguishing him from the amateur is the number of tools at his disposal, not the tools themselves. When something is available to everybody, it becomes common, ordinary. The same is true for wheelbarrows, sickles, and pruning shears: all the same design, they usually come from a single distant factory. This sort of equipment is never maintained—it is used and then thrown out. What does it matter? The same object, equally functional and unappealing, is still stocked in a warehouse somewhere. The same is the case for sprayers—identical and interchangeable, they are often considered disposable. Moreover, they seem to be on their way out, replaced by large tanks, also in plastic. The gardeners used to paint them with the colors of their favorite teams and show them off like trophies. Today they get rid of them before they're even broken. Sadness is born of uniformity.

As gardening techniques changed, other practices have also disappeared. I'm probably among the last active in my field to have once known some of them, and I'd like to dedicate a few lines to their memory, before they're forgotten for good. Special sickles and knives called *serpes* and *serpettes* were once used to clean wounded trees. It may sound strange, but grafts, a traditional practice that all amateur gardeners have usually tried at least once, hardly exist anymore—most plants are purchased already grafted, leaving *serpettes* abandoned in the cupboard. The *serpe* is one of the oldest tools in the world. The Greeks used it as a symbol of intelligence, at once sharp and curved. I particularly like how its form reminds me of a question mark. The *serpe* was useful whenever delicate precision was in order—for separating two branches, removing a single plant from a crowded border, or removing an overeager tendril of ivy. Versailles once had an impressive collection of all different models, with handles made of boxwood, horn, or ivory. Today, they slumber in some dusty cellar and will one day disappear, like the watering cans from the time of Louis XVI that I once came across by chance. Farewell to the clever *serpe*, farewell to the *échenilloirs* (pole pruning saws), *greffoirs* (grafting knives), *grattoirs*, and *ébran-choirs* (long-handled pruning shears). Farewell willow baskets, braided baskets, convex or concave, where impeccable rows of strawberries once slept. Farewell, too, to the myriad objects that once served at harvest time, apple pickers, asparagus knives, and other harvesting tools. Now giant machines clutch the tree's trunk and shake it, like the victim of a violent interrogation, until all of the fruit has fallen. Generally speaking, every specially adapted tool that once allowed meticulous finesse, by hook or by crook, has been swept away. Handshears have been replaced by electric or motorized hedge trimmers that make it difficult to choose which branches will get the whack. How can one steer a vibrating blade? We no longer prune the trees and bosquets, we hack them back—and no special tool is needed for such cruel work. What purpose do we have anymore for the fine-bladed *taupières* or the broad-bladed laurel shears? Farewell then, obsolete objects whose time has passed. Who knows? Perhaps one day another gardener will tenderly look back on his old Kubota tractor and his trusty leaf blower.

On my first day of work, I was given a hoe and told to work the earth in a parterre. The shovel, spading fork, and rake are the gardener's three most useful tools. With these three instruments and a bit of experience, it is possible to complete almost any chore. It's simple to hoe, even childish, everyone agrees, and so did I, until the day I started trying it. My debut was a disaster—I beat the earth in wild gestures, as though taming a beast, receiving only blisters and a backache in return. When I was done, the parterre looked like a trench. In spite of myself, and without really realizing it, I had discovered the value of apprenticeship and teamwork.

Our days began with everybody gathered together in the courtyard, where individual tasks were assigned. We met while the sun was still rising, Choron standing in the center and ranting at those who leaned on the handles of their rakes or hoes, inspecting uniforms (blue overalls and a cap marked with the letters PN for *parcs nationaux*, of which we were proud), congratulating some and calling out others. What with the masculine camaraderie, the uniforms, the stubbornness of some and the rebelliousness of others, the working-class men and the veterans, and a mission to accomplish, I often remembered *The Bridge on the River Kwai*—the only thing missing was the music. I whistled the movie's theme song at work one day, earning a certain respect from my colleagues, a chorus of laughter among the troops, and a reprimand from Choron, probably wounded by the comparison between his jolly, round French figure and the stolid Lieutenant Colonel of the film, Alec Guinness. Those morning meetings were also the occasion to drink the first coffee of the day, a coffee that many of my colleagues thinned with a splash of liquor from miniscule bottles, illegibly labeled and kept close, inside breast pockets, for the length of the day.

In those days, gardeners were among the "virile" professionals. They smoked and drank in the morning! Just as men from good families preferred English cigarettes, and cowboys Marlboros, the gardener of Versailles passed the day smoking unfiltered Boyards, one puff of which would make anybody else ill. The average gardener could talk and work with the butt still clenched in the corner of his mouth. He lit his cigarette, wedged it between his lips, from which it no longer moved, spat into his palms (a real talent when one already has a cigarette in one's mouth), and picked up his spade. The gardener generally lived in the park, a place he knew like the back of his hand. He had a wife, whom he referred to as his "old woman," but for whom he was willing to do anything.

At nine in the morning, the crew took a short break to eat This meal was and is a veritable institution. Theirs was physical work, and I guarantee you that if you spend three hours sawing a tree trunk or moving logs, you get hungry. The gardener, unfortunately, was often also a poacher and was hardly an expert in etiquette. I found an internal memo dated February 1961 from the head of the garden crew to his men, deploring their "complete lack of manners" and reminding them that "politeness requires that when somebody enters a room, especially *Monsieur le Curateur*, one rises and says *bonjour*."

The gardeners were most often from rural backgrounds; many of them didn't finish school—as a result they were little informed about polite behavior. I remember that in my early days, one of the first pieces of advice I received (from one of the old-timers who had probably been a victim of the note from

1961) was that I should stand as soon as I saw a "superior." These are my impressions of my first mornings working at Versailles. It's hard to believe that today my gardeners drink tea, don't smoke, and chew chlorophyll gum!

Given my lack of natural talent, Choron, whom I hadn't yet dared to make fun of, remarked, "Well, now we know you're no good with a hoe," making the others laugh. Through some sort of alchemy that I still can't explain, he also opened the door to my acceptance as part of the team. Up until then, I had always felt excluded, at a distance from the others—then all of a sudden, I was integrated into the group. He could have shouted, "He's one of us now," and it would have been just as clear. From that point onward, work was no longer tiresome—the other gardeners talked to me, and there was always somebody willing to show me the movements I should use, to tell me that if I worked in one position or another I would end up with a backache, or to show me how to better distribute the weight to conserve my strength. Work was still a struggle—I even remember being told that I wasn't allowed to complain about my blisters anymore—but I sensed that my efforts weren't in vain and that I was learning. And besides, unlike most of my earlier years, I was now with people who were supportive. When your hands are cut up, crippled by cramps, and raw with blisters, the words "the trade is sinking in," are a comfort, if not a remedy. The work I was given was simple, but one had to know a number of little "tricks" to do it well.

These aren't the sorts of things one learns in books or accumulates with multiple diplomas; rather, one needs know-how, at once simple and very human, and that requires a certain apprenticeship. I'm not a believer in correspondence courses! In horticulture, you are not merely taught, you are trained under the watchful eye of an experienced gardener, who corrects you and shows you thousands of tricks of the trade. Our knowledge is transmitted more than taught—perhaps this is the privilege of the professions that are referred to, often with a touch of condescension, as "manual." On the contrary, I think the manual aspect of our work is a sign of superiority—what could be more beautiful than knowing how to use one's own hands?

The paleontologist André Leroi-Gourhan affirmed that language was the result of our ability to use our hands: "The hand liberated the word." The hypothesis according to which the human capacity for thought results from this same manual aptitude is largely accepted—our intelligence as a species is the result of our opposable thumbs. I don't know whether this scientific theory is really the case, but I'm often surprised at our scorn for what is one of the noblest parts of our body. The palms of our hands contain the whole of humanity, not to mention our individuality. Fingerprints are the only external trait that allows a man to be identified for the entire length of his life, and some even believe that our destiny can be read in the lines on our palms.

I don't have much taste for (and even less faith in) palm reading, but I love the infinite individuality of hands. I like how hands betray our age, excitability, and even hobbies. Like many of my colleagues, I love observing, and for me, hands are the clearest path to investigating the human soul. The short, crude hands of a woman who spends her Sundays making pottery; the twisted, shameful, and dented fingers of an otherwise beautiful woman; the splayed, yellowed phalanges of a cigar smoker; the mangled cuticles of a nervous teenager; the smooth bump on the middle finger of writers and teachers—these striking details have helped me to understand more than one situation.

In a way, it's like learning to recognize a plant: each detail is the sign of a particular characteristic. As a child, I remember contemplating my grandfather's hands—there was his paralyzed hand, yellow and somewhat shrunken with atrophy, and on the other side, both older and more alive, his gardener's hand. The lines on his face have long since changed in my mind's eye, but I only have to close my eyes to see his hands: the veins, the skin, parchmentlike, slightly violet and swollen, the short and extraordinarily hard nails (I think at the end of his life, he used a pair of pruning shears to cut them), streaked with little white marks and blackened at the tips, much to my grandmother's dismay. I imagined, just as the highest and most venerable mountains are always capped with snow, that my grandfather's fingers must have always been covered in eternal earth. In spite of my suits and life as a businessman, I always have mangled fingernails.

I feel sorry for the apprentice gardeners of today. I think that we don't know how to teach the manual trades any longer, and gardening is now taught the same way as math or philosophy! If it is true, as some say, that gardens are often conducive to philosophy, the inverse situation is rarely the case. You will learn little of a trade shut up in a library, reading manuals and writing papers on the art and manner of planting cabbage. It is a noble intention to cultivate equality in opportunities and knowledge, but it is just as important to recognize the diverse forms that knowledge can assume. The worst part of this otherwise generous quest for equality has resulted in a uniformity of teaching methods. France is obsessed with hierarchy—and the model for educating gardeners has followed that of other disciplines, even the most "noble" and intellectual of them. Equality gives way to norms and conformity (traits to which I have an aversion), which means that French diplomas in gardening are a failure.

What is the result of all of these fancy diplomas in my gardens? My apprentices know their botany textbooks backwards and forwards, but they are incapable of recognizing a plant when it is found in the garden instead of on a computer screen.

Paradoxically, as species and cultivars become better catalogued, it has become harder and harder for gardeners to keep abreast of the plants in existence: one knows less because there is more to know. Moreover, I believe our profession is one of observation—we must see and touch the plant in order to know it. How is this possible in the case of exotic plants? And certain plants proliferate at a staggering pace. The fashion for new hybrids means that there are dozens of new varieties every year. It has become a problem even for me—not only do I have to keep up to speed, but should I have the misfortune of becoming attached to a particular variety, there is no guarantee that I'll be able to find the same seeds a few years down the line. Roses are the best example of this. You like the variety "Catherine Deneuve"? Well, two hundred other hybrids have already replaced it...the renown of actresses themselves is less ephemeral! These modern flowers are also more fragile and sterile: they don't produce viable seeds. You'll never find volunteer seedlings of hybrid scented stock or Pompadour roses in the countryside around Versailles.

When La Quintinie wanted to gather more information on a particular plant species, he took his botany manual and went out into the gardens. On a plot of ground as large as Versailles, he was bound to find what he was looking for; and if he didn't, he would add a line to his manual upon returning home, according to the nature of his discovery.

One of the rare privileges of my age is that I am part of the last generation to have used Gaston Bonnier's *Nouvelle Flore*, once the go-to guide for apprentice gardeners. The "Bonnier," although austere and stodgy, defined plants according to their characteristics. A plant with alternating and non-stipulate leaves and epigynous flowers had to be a daisy. The terms seem complex, but they described simple, precise cases. Identification was simple—you read honorable Gaston, then you looked at the flower, counted the number of petals, observed its shape, along with the shape of the leaves, and with all of these details in mind, you could identify the flower. The answer was always within reach, but it had to be earned. Now nature walks and plant guides have been replaced by the photographs in manuals that are as voluminous as they are unwieldy, and most recently, by electronic media. Thanks to technology, there is no longer any need to go out into nature—a strange sort of progress indeed, remaining shut indoors instead of walking through a garden. Moreover, in a photo, one has little idea of the size of a plant. (One of my apprentice gardeners will always be remembered for confusing a crocus and a magnolia!) Although the number of species seems infinite, the amount of money that publishers of guides can spend on illustrations is limited—for each sort of plant or flower that is shown, one would need not just a manual, no matter how thick and heavy, but also a twenty-volume ency-clopedia! For example, there are over fifty different sorts of oak trees—but no guide prints fifty photos of the same variety of tree. Even supposing that this problem were resolved, how will the budding gardener tell the difference between an oak and an ash in the winter? Today's instruction is far too theoretical, and as a consequence, deceptive. Many of a gardener's jobs require little specialization. With their fancy diplomas in hand, it feels like betrayal when they come face-to-face with the reality of the job. This is easily understood, and I don't resent my interns—I simply regret that they have been duped by the system.

I like the idea of apprenticeship—not out of a taste for the past, but because it makes it clear that it takes time to learn. An act has to be learned far more slowly than a mathematical formula. The hand and the body take more time than the intellect. How many times must we repeat a movement, however simple, in order to master it? It takes years to learn to play the piano, for the hand to learn and incorporate the knowledge entrusted to it—so why is it thought that a month (the time given to most garden interns) is enough to educate a gardener? Know-how is imbued with an incredible nonchalance—in the garden, it may be far simpler, but it is certainly far slower than mere knowledge. It takes time to master movements, and even longer to understand their consequences. It is rare that such things are instantaneously evident, particularly in our profession. It takes years for a tree to reach maturity. Knowing whether a tree is healthy or not is only evident at the end of a year, sometimes two. If you want to find out whether the tree you have just planted will grow to be beautiful, you must wait fifteen years.

Nothing is more beautiful, in my opinion, than caring for a tree. Unlike flowers, trees are maintained over a long period of time. They are necessary—they maintain the quality of the earth, renew the air, shelter wildlife, and in some cases, mask an ugly view. A flower is ephemeral—it appears in spring and dies a few months later—whereas a tree is a lasting part of its environment. Above all else, a tree has a past—when Katrina uprooted the oaks on Lousiana's old plantations, a living page of history was ripped from the books.

Slowness is an integral part of my profession—the snails chosen by Le Nôtre for his coat of arms were a humorous manner of underlining this essential truth. This is why the recent technological revolution in gardening has hardly been a success. Technology has permitted a fair share of miracles, but not in gardens. Work done quickly isn't beneficial because nature itself is slow. In the end, it's a simple question of rhythm and harmony. What is the point in doing things more quickly?

A few years ago, I was invited to a wedding in Cameroon. The jungle was fabulous—immense trees as far as the eye could see, full of the racket of monkeys and parrots. I was with a friend who insisted we take a car so that we could get the trip out of the way in a day. In the end, all I saw of Cameroon was a highway, similar to the highways that we have in France. At the party on the evening following the wedding, I talked with a young man who told me he had just walked the same distance, but through the forest, and that it had taken him two days. I may have traveled more quickly, but I know quite well who wasted their time.

The Versailles of my youth is gone now, and I know that there's no use in nursing regrets. If I'm happy to have known the last days of that bygone era, I am just as pleased that the gardens have become an attractive, modern undertaking, to which I contribute, and that I hope I have helped to improve.

# M

≈≈≈

I LIVE IN Molière's former house. Knowing that I also once lived in one of André Malraux's dwellings, I can only blush at my own literary inclinations! The Régie du Trianon, which I have occupied since 1982, is, apart from the château, the oldest building on the domain. It dates from the period of the Trianon de Porcelaine, which no longer exists. Few people realize it, but the domain of Versailles also includes a number of little buildings hidden in the depths of the woods—these are the homes occupied by the personnel of Versailles and their families. My home is an attractive building that opens directly to the outdoors; the worm-eaten wood of the front door indicates its advanced age. The structure also once served as a stable and is accessed by a twisting path, as inconvenient by car as on foot. It is modest when compared to the exuberant luxury of the neighboring structures, and I appreciate it all the more for its modesty. Grand homes in marble and gilt leave me cold. I enjoy admiring them, but I wouldn't want to live in one—they look too much like movie sets. Even the Maison du Jardinier, built under Louis XV for Claude Richard, is too grand—a veritable country mansion graciously offered by the king to his valet. I greatly prefer the

Régie du Trianon, even if it looks more rustic, as it was given over to no particular function. Set apart on a broad lawn, not far from the Trianon itself, it has an ideal placement—I'm at once at the heart of the park and independent from it.

Dusk here is beautiful. On certain occasions, my wife and I walk down to the gardens of the Trianon to drink a glass of champagne on one of the magnificent marble benches that ornament the grounds. We chat and contemplate the impressive spectacle of the château lit up by the day's final rays of sunlight. These are sweet, gentle hours, favorable to happiness and daydreaming. We tell each other about the insignificant details of our respective days; in the distance we can hear ice cubes clinking in other glasses, as the Trianon itself disappears in the orange haze of sunset. I love these moments, both exceptional and regular—they are one of the greatest privileges that Versailles has offered me. On the nights of galas held at the Trianon, I admire the lights of the party, like that given upon the arrival of the year 2000 by a Greek arms dealer. The Trianon often hosts receptions given by our donors or the government, but it is rarely rented to a private party. The billionaire had risen to the height of the honor that had been granted him: the party, it was said, was splendid. I don't often attend such receptions, because it is rare that a gardener is invited, but also because I know that the view from my house is even better. There is no better spot in Versailles to watch fireworks at the Trianon than from my own living room! While the rich and powerful of the world, suffocating in their suits or shivering in their dresses, are blinded by the fireworks that they have to crane their necks to admire, we watch on, comfortable among our friends, whom I never forget to invite for these occasions. The ability to reconcile château life and country life is not the least among the advantages of my job!

Molière wasn't invited to the grand events of Versailles either. He was a servant, and the fact that he was housed in what, in those days, was a stable, says a great deal about his status at Versailles. He stayed here rarely, but he left behind, for the centuries to come, his humor and intelligence. Beyond his literary genius, of which I am doubtlessly not the best judge, I have a great deal of admiration for Molière the man. Of all the great names attached to Versailles, his (along with La Fontaine, perhaps) is by far the one I prefer. Who else would have dared, before an audience of devoted men of the church, headed up by Conti and the pious Queen Mother, to perform a play such as *Tartuffe*? The performance created a scandal and the work was banned, but Molière refused to change a single line. Rejecting a future as a courtier, he preferred to keep his independence and humor. May the "demon clothed in flesh," as the doctors of the Sorbonne referred to him, ever watch over me!

Molière is also attached to one of my personal memories. In 1977 I was still a young gardener assigned to the least appealing chores in the garden. One of my jobs was to remove all the fallen leaves from the allées and bosquets before the public arrived in the gardens. Since the park opened at eight in the morning, I was already at work at dawn. As the cool morning seeped into my body. I went about my work in peace, when suddenly, I heard voices behind the bushes. I hadn't been at Versailles for long, but the old gardeners had already told me all the bloody and passionate stories that had unfolded in the park. Though they had assuredly taken pleasure in embellishing the stories with romantic details, they also told me how I ought to behave should I come across something suspicious. I advanced, spade in hand like a spear, toward the Bosquet de la Reine, from which I had heard the strange sounds. I hesitated for a moment, wondering whether I shouldn't call upon my colleagues, but my curiosity got the better of me. A charming spectacle revealed itself from behind the curtain of shrubbery. About twenty men and women, wearing period costumes, occupied the space. Among them, a man was reciting a text with great passion. He turned around—it was Molière, the same man whose portrait could be found in the texts of classic French literature I had studied in high school. "Laurent, lock up my hair shirt with my whip," he proclaimed, looking in my direction, without seeming to see me. He hardly lifted his head, and it felt as though he was speaking to somebody standing directly behind me. I was astonished to see that none of his colleagues interrupted my arrival. Had they seen me? Yet it seemed as though a woman with dark hair had given me a knowing smile. For a few minutes, I remained under the spell, refusing to believe what I was seeing, until a man wearing too much makeup said something, concerned about the coffee going cold.

Suddenly, the anonymous, unknown outdoor scenery melted into the familiar Bosquet de la Reine, and the alexandrines gave way to the latest slang. Although I'm usually observant, it was only then that I noticed the tennis shoes and modern watchbands underneath the gowns. The seventeenth century evaporated. The Molière I had just encountered was none other than the character created by Ariane Mnouchkine. He wasn't famous yet, but he had just won over his first fan before even releasing the film. From then on, whenever I had the opportunity, I watched every detail of the film shoot. One of the most beautiful moments was a scene shot on the grand staircase leading to the château— the entire troupe (which I had come to feel as though I knew, having so often watched them rehearse) descended the stairs of the Orangerie hand in hand. It seemed as though the theater had created a big family—which I doubt—but it's true that I don't have many positive memories of my own family. Still, the few weeks I spent in the company of the Théâtre du Soleil gave me a taste for their art. When I saw them on the stairs, I was both their spectator and their partner. Behind them, fireworks lit up the sky. From the top of the stairs, the fictitious troupe, played by cinema actors, bowed to an imaginary public. Through this gesture, the director gave homage to Versailles, to history, and to the theater.

Countless films have been shot at Versailles. In the seventeenth century, Lully, La Fontaine, and Racine clamored to offer their talents to the king. Today it is Depardieu, Coppola, and

Mnouchkine who come to honor Versailles or in search of its prestige. So many famous names have come here, that the choice of working at Versailles itself feels like a sort of celebration. A dialogue has been created between the artists of yesteryear and those of today. I think that many of the painters, writers, and actors that I have witnessed at Versailles have come in search of their ancestors. There is nothing so meaningful for a writer as to walk down the allées where Rousseau, Racine, Chateaubriand, Musset, and so many others once strolled; for a painter to see the effects of light that once inspired Poussin or the exteriors upon which Hubert Robert once based his fantasies; for an actor to see the house in which Molière once lived. This is a way of placing oneself in the continuity of history and rendering homage to a series of one's spiritual artistic ancestors. I think this is why so many of today's artists, from Piccoli to Serrault, from Elton John to Claudia Cardinale, from Madonna to Michael Jackson, have made a stop in the gardens of Versailles. Many of them come for a shoot, only to return in secret, to make a more personal and anonymous nod; I once came across Nicole Kidman, who, deep in the park, was reading on a bench on a fine autumn day.

Versailles is more than just a film set—(if this were not the case, a clever builder or a special effect would suffice, or even present a more convincing illusion of the past). What do these artists seek in Versailles? More than a frame, I think they are looking for an atmosphere—the stones, trees, and colors carry a message that no history book is capable of transmitting and that only the experience of a visit or even better, a stay, allows one to understand. It is up to the artist to be sufficiently receptive. This is not always simple. People often believe that life at Versailles was frozen in place the day the king left, but in reality, the château and its gardens have evolved a great deal from the time of Marie Antoinette! Louis-Philippe, in particular, brought about a certain number of modifications, the most important of which was the construction of the Galerie des Batailles, as did Napoleon before him. The park, too, has changed, especially since the storm of 1999. Marie Antoinette would have trouble recognizing the massive trunk that has lain on the ground in front of the Trianon since the drought of 2003 though it was the frail young oak tree that once offered her its shade! I love it when the park is full of coquettish Marquises or fearsome revolutionaries for a movie shoot—it feels like a snapshot of what the park once saw long ago is being offered up anew.

It's thanks to these film shoots that I became interested in the history of France, and especially in the history of the park. One of my missions has been to assure or verify the "botanical coherence" of certain scenes. What were the flowers and trees that the queen once contemplated? Film crews are increasingly demanding in this respect, and I recall one scene that, happily, has escaped immortalization. The park is often filmed for brief images used between two scenes filmed elsewhere—these are by far the most common images shot. On the day in question, the gardens received the crew of Miloš Forman, whose film *Valmont*

208 | THE GARDENER OF VERSAILLES

required a few extra exterior shots. I had been informed on the previous day that one of the parterres was to be used. The director had asked for a charming country lawn, and I was pleased not only because of my own personal preference for this sort of lawn, but also because the choice corresponded to a historical reality: Forman had made an informed decision.

The first day of filming came off without a hitch. Between meetings, I managed to watch some of the filming. Everything took place in incredible silence. It is interesting to note how much the atmosphere of a shoot is determined by a film's director. People were always bursting into laughter on the set of *Danton*, although it was hardly a comedy, whereas, with Forman, things were very quiet and serious.

The following day, before work, as I was on my way to admire some flighty countesses, or at least their amiable servants, I was alarmed to smell the odor of freshly cut grass. When I arrived on-site, the drama had already begun—on the newly even grass, in the place of a marquise, Forman stood alone, screaming in Czech. Against my orders, one of my crew had decided to mow the lawn. He had meant well, but he had rendered useless all of the footage shot the previous day. I tried to explain what had happened but received only a stream of insults, first in English, then in Czech. I may not be talented when it comes to languages, but the gist of what was being said didn't escape me, and the Queen of the Night's high note had nothing on the shrieking of the director of *Amadeus*. Forman was livid. With a sheepish smile, I vainly tried to get a word in edgewise. It was by far the funniest scene from the film! It's a pity it ended up on the cutting room floor.

Generally speaking—this is something I've noticed at Versailles—film directors are increasingly painstaking when it comes to detail. When I think of the fastidious Sofia Coppola, who asked for the same waterlilies as those seen in a particular etching, and compare her approach with the crude errors and clumsy continuity of Sacha Guitry in his 1954 *Royal Affairs in Versailles*, I find myself seeing two different models of movie-making. Although Guitry's film has admirable qualities, and did much for the garden's reputation, it is packed full of historical errors. The lawns are cut short, the trees are far too tall and mature, and the flowering chestnuts date from a period well after the scenes he portrays. These inexactitudes don't bother me—on the contrary, they are one of the film's charming details and even help me in my work to know more about the state of the gardens in the 1950s. Here again, Versailles opened a door, allowing me a backstage view of cinematic art, one I had long admired.

IT IS SAID that all roads lead to Rome, but in my opinion, they first take a detour through Versailles. In my years at Versailles, it seems as though not one of the great men and women of the world has missed visiting the allées of the château, whether on a state or personal visit. Many don't realize it, but Versailles has continued to play a role in political history. French parliamentary life first saw the light of day at the château under Louis XVI, when the delegates of the Third Estate took on the title of the *Assemblée nationale*, before pledging the Tennis Court Oath in the Salle de Jeu de Paume on June 20, 1789. Contemporary France was born at Versailles. It was within the same walls, at Versailles, in 1885, that the Republic was consolidated with the voting of the Wallon Amendment, establishing the democratic election of French presidents. The treaty ending the First World War was signed in Versailles. And Versailles continues to be the site where the two houses of the French legislature meet to vote joint referendums when they are united in a single congress. Since de Gaulle, an entire wing of the Grand Trianon has been reserved for use by the French president. Somewhat paradoxically, of all the presidents of the Fifth Republic, it was the socialist François Mitterrand who most relished this particular privilege. His supporters saw in this a sign of his good taste, his detractors an indication of hypocrisy. As I recall it, his presence felt by far the most "royal."

My duties are relatively few when it comes to official ceremonies, limited to, at most, leading a tour of the gardens. I can hardly complain: I'm not one for cosmopolitan events. I have a particularly bad memory of the G7 Summit that took place in the château in 1982. Everything was locked down, searched, and guarded—returning to my own house felt like crossing the Iron Curtain. Once I was even refused access to my own house because I had forgotten my identity papers when I took my dog for a walk. The lawn alongside the Grande Allée had been requisitioned to serve as a landing pad, with the sheep continuing to graze between the waiting helicopters. Versailles felt like a war zone. The noise was particularly unbearable, and it made me wonder how Reagan, Thatcher, and Mitterrand had avoided going deaf.

Once the initial curiosity of seeing world leaders with your own eyes wears off, boredom is not long in following. The most surprising part of these sightings is the sudden appearance of a media celebrity in one's ordinary daily life. I know it sounds childish, but to me, the president of the United States is somebody who lives primarily on CNN, in a shadowy and mythical world somewhere between reality and the imaginary—certainly not in *my* world. Yet the king of Morocco, Reagan, Gorbachev, George and Barbara Bush, Fidel Castro, and, of course, the French presidents, from Giscard to Chirac, have all walked past my windows.

I particularly remember a surprise morning meeting with Boris Yeltsin. I was leaving my house earlier than usual, because on the days of official ceremonies, the gardens are under surveillance from dawn, with the château becoming a Massada-like citadel. Seated on my doorstep, a man in a suit was watching the sunrise. I was surprised that security had let a visitor enter the park—then I recognized the massive silhouette of the Russian president. He rose to his feet, seeming as startled as I felt. He muttered a few words in his beautiful language, of which I understood nothing at all.

I thought a walk in the park would help him wake up, so I talked to him about the flowers and trees and everything else that I loved at Versailles. He didn't understand me, of course, but just hearing another voice helps a person to concentrate. I felt a strange satisfaction in speaking to my silent companion. I put so much passion into my story that I felt as though he was starting to take interest. I saw a sincere smile start to dawn on his face when I pointed out a tree that I particularly cherished. As strange as it might seem, we understood each other. My plan worked perfectly—once we arrived at the château, his official personality returned. The gardens had brought us closer, allowing him to live a few moments of peace in the midst of his frenetic schedule—allowing me to finally be heard. After this exchange, we parted ways.

Malraux referred to the great names that pepper history without having greatly altered it as "passing guests." I wouldn't be surprised if that phrase came to him during his stay at Versailles. The château's guestbook contains such a great number of prestigious names that any single man, no matter how great, will always be inferior to the sum of all those who signed before him and who will one day sign after him. Faced with this encyclopedia of great personalities, one is overwhelmed with an impression of one's own fleeting futility. At Versailles, only the stones are eternal.

Malraux understood this well, when as de Gaulle's minister, he lived in the Pavillon de la Lanterne. I know the spot, for I was housed there during my military service. A sort of miniature château, the term *"lanterne"* refers, in architecture, to rooms that are open to the outside on both sides. One enters La Lanterne through a high gate decorated with stags' heads. The spot is intimate, cut off from the outside world, and it possesses a gracious, feminine charm. The house, with its small, pure proportions, carefully chiseled profile, and soft colors recalls the charming and infantile beauty of paintings by Fragonard and Boucher. La Lanterne is like a delicately dressed little noblewoman. From his retreat, Malraux wrote about the various great events of the world beyond, and the small, daily pleasures of living at Versailles—as much about political reflections on a new world taking shape as about the cats that walked upon the stags' heads decorating the gate, or the happiness of his nearly daily encounters with a little hedgehog. Malraux wondered whether the ancestors of the little animal might have witnessed the events of the Revolution; he wondered what had happened to the animals in the nearby Ménagerie after the end of the monarchy. He imagined, with humor, the museum employees chasing butterflies and hunting down the last camel. In reading these admirable pages, I sense the gentleness, peace, and depth that can be drawn from the place. Malraux knew how to put into words the strange mix of feelings that Versailles evokes. What does the noise and flash of those sparring for power matter when their renown will never change that of Versailles? Watching the endless parades and processions, the walls of the place seem to mutter haughtily, "Of all these great names, none will live forever." At Versailles we are all "passing guests."

To me, the great names of Versailles are not those of the presidents that honor us with their visits—my portrait gallery is far more modest. First, there are those who love the gardens, anonymous or famous, whose daily presence is a veritable homage. I think of Marcel, who has come to the gardens for fifteen years to smoke the delicious cigar that his doctors—with the support of his wife—have formally forbidden. Marcel has a particular bench and time of day, and he always greets me with the same knowing gesture. There is the orchid collector who always tells me about his latest discoveries, and Michelle, who asks me every year whether I would like to join the Association Marie-Antoinette. They have become so familiar that their presence gives a rhythm to my work. If I don't run into the beautiful jogger in her blue headband, I know I'm late. The woman with the little dog is a sign that it will soon be lunchtime. Marcel's cigar announces the end of the day, and the honking horn of the man who rents the bicycles tells me it is time to head home. The appearance of the ice cream vendor means that warm weather is on the way, just as surely as the hatching of the cygnets or the first blooming flowers, and the increasing bad humor among my crew is a sure sign of approaching winter and the first frost. This is the time of the year I dislike the most, when the trees lose their leaves and transform themselves into skeletons. Versailles becomes macabre, until the following spring, and I think of Mallarmé, another familiar name, who once haunted Versailles, coming to bury his cats in the depths of the park, with the complicit approval of Marras, the curator in those days. To accompany these gloomy ceremonies, Marras turned on all of the fountains, while Mallarmé recited a toast in honor of the deceased animal. Molière, Malraux, Mallarmé—these three great writers have guided me through the riches of this place. May these lines be considered a fleeting homage to them, as well as to all the other lovers of Versailles.

# PLEASURES AND DAYS
≈≈≈≈≈≈≈≈≈≈≈≈≈≈≈≈≈≈≈≈≈≈≈

ALL CASTLES HOUSE princesses, who require balls for dancing, jousts to impress them, and stories to make them dream. Versailles is no exception to this rule—as well as being a seat of power, the domain has long been a place of festivity. The classic, austere facade sometimes causes us to forget it, but Versailles once served and still serves as the setting for sumptuous spectacles and celebrations. The court had to be amused at Versailles during the time of Louis XIV; such distractions were even the center of social life at the château. With a few exceptions, the nobility in those days was young, for people didn't live very long. They were also rich, and, of course, idle. Not only did the French aristocrat not have to work, he was *expected* not to work. If one managed to reach what we call adulthood, but which, at the time, was the equivalent of old age, one had all the time in the world for plotting or slander, unless, in repenting for a sinful past, one had already fallen into religious devotion. What else was there to do? In the past, scheming and par-tying were the primary activities at Versailles. I'll leave it to sharper tongues to claim that the tradition continues to this day.

The very idea of Versailles was born at a party. When Louis XIII decided to build the château in 1623, he intended, according to a Venetian ambassador, to create *"una piccola casa per ricreazione,"* in short, a folly. If the *"casa"* hardly remained *"piccola,"* the ambassador was right—Louis XIII's peaceful country retreat was not long in becoming the site of elaborate equestrian parades and fireworks. The fate of the château was sealed at a party that took place, not at Versailles, but Vaux-le-Vicomte, on an August evening of 1661. Nicolas Fouquet's heraldic symbol was the squirrel—and this descendant of a long line of ministers had, over the course of the years, squirreled away one of the largest fortunes in the kingdom. As is often the way with thrifty families, there eventually comes an extravagant son or some other shameful relation to squander the carefully acquired fortune in a sort of natural regulation of wealth; one thinks of the highly likeable examples of Uncle Bachelard in Emile Zola's *Pot-Bouille* or the incomparable Pierre Brasseur and his role in Denys de la Pattellière's 1958 film, *Les Grandes Familles*.

In the case of Fouquet, it was not women who led to his ruin, but the arts—he was an aesthete to his bones and Vaux-le-Vicomte was his courtesan. He quickly became a patron of all of the great artists of his time. (La Fontaine, Le Brun, and Molière all depended in one way or another upon the incredible generosity of the Superintendent of Finances.) Jean-Baptiste Colbert, the Controller-General of Finances, and the other important finance minister during this period, had grown wary of Fouquet's increasing power. Fouquet's wastefulness was enough to throw a frugal man such as Colbert into cold sweats (it is said that the models for La Fontaine's version of the fable "The Grasshopper and the Ant" were Fouquet and Colbert), but it also gave Colbert a grain of hope. He was delighted when the young Louis XIV, jealous of such splendor, decided to imprison his arrogant minister after the famous party at Vaux-le-Vicomte. Colbert's triumph was short-lived, however, for Louis XIV was as quick to spend money as his former Superintendent. The Baroque munificence introduced by Fouquet was not condemned to disappear; it simply changed hands. The grasshopper of fable became royal, disillusioning ants like Colbert.

The first fête given at Versailles was, strictly speaking, a rehearsal: The *Impromptu de Versailles* of 1663. Because nothing had yet changed at the château (the construction was barely underway), the object of the celebration was the ephemeral itself. Temporary decors covered up the construction work and were burned afterwards, while on the stage—the very epitome of evanescence—Molière told the story of an impossible rehearsal for which the actors didn't even have time to learn their roles. The court, which had been invited to admire the grand renovations to the château, was dazzled. The Ménagerie made a particularly strong impression, with the nobility crowded into its large octagonal salon to admire a variety of exotic animals in total security. What a strange sight it must have been, somewhat premonitory even, the rows of aristocrats lined up to contemplate gazelles, ostriches, and elephants as captive as they were splendidly decorated. Twenty years later, Louis XIV would encage the court itself.

In another spectacle, Roger, a courageous knight astride a hippogriff, has just saved the beautiful Angélique. The sorceress Alcine entraps him upon an enchanted island, but Roger manages to overcome her spell. A princess, a young and handsome knight, and the magic of a woman as wise as she was smitten—what better emblems could Louis XIV, that prince who seemed to have been born under a lucky star, have chosen? Louis XIV's Angélique was none other than Louise de la Vallière. The king was only twenty-five years old, and was still keeping his romantic affair secret—but to celebrate La Vallière, he organized *"The Pleasures of the Enchanted Island, gallant and magnificent feasts given by the King,"* in May of 1664.

From the outside, the celebrations seemed no more than the king's desire to amuse his subjects and be distracted alongside them. The play was met with such great success that the program, from the description of the costumes, sets, and theater, down to the text, with its plot and annexes, was published in its entirety, with illustrations engraved by Israël Silvestre.[13]

*The King, wishing to give to the Queens and all his Court, the pleasure of a few extraordinary fêtes in a place decorated with all of the amenities that might cause one to admire a country house, chose Versailles, four leagues*

---

13. The following citations are drawn from this anonymous text.

*from Paris. This is a château that one might describe as an*
*enchanted palace—so much have the adjustments of art*
*effectively seconded the care with which nature sought to*
*render the site perfect.*

The young king's exploit was to have elevated simple pleasure to the level of art. The festivities lasted more than a week,
attracting more than six thousand spectators from the capital. Ten
years after the *"piccola casa"* referred to by the Venetian ambassador, Versailles was no longer a poor cousin to the Carnival of
Venice. Gondolas offered by the doge himself rocked gently on
the waters of Versailles's Grand Canal, surrounded by reduced-
scale galleons, galliots, and brigantines—a miniature navy.
Versailles itself had become a "little Venice."

The ceremonies opened on the evening of May 7 with an
equestrian parade. In those times, the horse was at the heart of
social life and a symbol of nobility. Gentlemen were expected to
be good horsemen, to hunt and ride with grace. One of the most
popular numbers in these spectacles was the *carrousel*—a sort
of descendant of medieval jousts meant to show off the physical prowess and elegance of rival courtiers. The most famous of
these was surely the one given in 1662, to celebrate the birth of
the Dauphin, in the heart of Paris on the public square that has
since been known as the Place du Carrousel. The noble horsemen paraded in sumptuous costumes, their horses decorated
in equal splendor. To indicate his triumph, the king paraded

alongside them, dressed as a Roman emperor and followed by a suite of two hundred men dressed in his colors. Imagine the sight of this column of men in gold, silver, and fire-red, parading upon the Place du Carrousel! Following behind, Monsieur (the king's brother), the Duke of Enghein, and the Prince of Condé directed a quadrille of different colors representing the kingdom of earth. Persians, Indians, Turks, and Americans were all arranged behind the fiery solar king of France, who had become the sun upon earth around which (since the time of Copernicus, at least) revolved the planets.

The *carrousel* of May 7, 1664, held at Versailles, was even more spectacular. A herald of arms appeared first, dressed in antique style. The poor boy must have been quivering in his toga, for he alone had been given the mission of opening the massive festivities before the entire court. I would bet that, given the costume, he felt not unlike one of the first Christian martyrs as he entered the arena. Behind him came a number of pages, d'Artagnan, and the Dukes of Noailles and Saint-Aignan. Upon the sound of twelve trumpets and four kettledrums, the king appeared, costumed as Roger himself. It was a veritable Hollywood epic! How did the king appear to those who saw him for the first time? Here is a sonnet composed in honor of the King Roger.

*What stature and carriage in this proud conqueror!*
*His presence dazzles whoever looks upon him,*
*And although his position is already grand,*

*Something more lights his face from within.*
*His brow bears proof of his august destiny:*
*His virtue surpasses that of his ancestors;*
*He causes us to forget them—and bringing fresh air,*
*He leaves his origins far behind.*

*From his generous heart, it is ordinary*
*For him to act on behalf of others before himself;*
*This is the primary occupation of his forces.*

*He eclipses the glory of ancient heroes,*
*Sees only honor, and only draws his sword*
*In the interest of others.*

Greater, stronger, nobler, and more generous—according to these lines, Louis XIV was assuredly the best of the best. The very essence of divine right, he surpassed even his ancestors. It must be said that after poverty and war on the one hand, and the Fronde on the other, the young king had every reason to want to distinguish himself from his predecessors. I don't pledge my faith to anybody, alas, not even to God, but the royal aura must have been exceptionally strong. Saint-Simon was forced to admit that "without the fear of the devil, which God left him even at his worst, he would have ordered men to adore him and would have found many willing to do so." The power wielded by Louis XIV was nearly mystical. Even the princes of the royal blood and the officers of the crown, the only men who had the remarkable honor of entering the royal apartments, bowed before his bed. In church, those present kneeled at the moment of the offertory; at Versailles, which did not initially have a chapel, those present bowed down at the moment of the king's official rising from bed. This etiquette, put in place during the reign of Louis XIV himself, became a sort of liturgy. If the use of the term *"etiquette"* in France dates to the rules set in place by Philip the Good, a Duke of Burgundy in the fifteenth century, it was only under Louis XIV that it truly triumphed. Its usefulness was, above all else, political. By governing the smallest details of the court and the king's daily life, the latter disciplined the former, keeping them occupied. Etiquette created a complex ceremony that became the object of every thought and conversation. Was it better to scratch or knock at a door? How could one slide across the château's parquet without making too much noise? Who had the right to be seated on a footstool in the presence of the king and queen? (This was a right usually reserved for those of high rank; others had to remain standing, of course.) Who had been refused the "honors of the Louvre," or the right to enter the courtyard of the king's residence in their own carriage? The schemers came to prefer to plot from beneath the protection of a polite smile, a graceful gesture, or a serious expression. The once-rebellious court was domesticated, become prisoner of daily rites and rituals. Versailles put the aristocracy on a short leash.

The courtier was kept busy from the *petit lever*, which took place in strictly limited company, to the public *grand coucher* in the evening. If he was one of the Great Officers of the Crown or the royal family itself (the king's worst possible rivals, for their ancestry allowed them to pretend succession to the crown itself), he was expected to attend the *petit lever*, dressed and powdered. While the king was still dozing, the high aristocracy was busy trying to look its best for the royal awakening. Perhaps it's because I'm more of a night owl, but it takes me a great deal of time and effort to be fresh first thing in the morning. In the early mornings of December, in particular, I'm sure more than one face bore the marks of the pillowcase instead of fresh powder.

If the courtier was of less elevated extraction, he would hurry instead to the public *grand lever*. Among hundreds of others, he waited in the Salon de l'Œil-de-bœuf, the antechamber to the public bedroom. When the doors opened, people pushed and shoved to be as close as possible to His Majesty. Standing before this barnyard full of aristocrats, the king would be dressed. His shirt was presented to him by the highest-ranking member of the royal family present on that day. To Louis XIV, whose pride had been wounded at the Louvre during his youth by the intrigues of the rebellious nobility, this scene must have brought a certain satisfaction. There was no better way to begin the day than with the sight of his rivals reduced to his servants.

Just a few hours separated the morning kowtowing from the queen's crossing the Hall of Mirrors at noon—followed by another crush of nobles eager to receive some sign of favor. The luckiest received a slight nod or smile. The royal couple, followed by the troop of courtiers, would go to the chapel. Though not tiny—it is Versailles after all—the chapel was still not large enough to accommodate everybody. As a result, only the king entered the holy sanctuary—interposing his services, in a sense, between God and man. What did it matter? The others had come not to pray but to watch the king pray for them. Here, too, the slightest gesture was the object of an infinitely complicated hierarchy—a chosen few had the right to a *carreau* or "cushion," but only the royal princes had a cloth thrown over their *prie-dieux*. No sooner was the mass finished than the crown rushed to the *petit couvert* served in the king's bedroom. Of course there was no question of eating, not even a buffet; there was merely the sight of the royal jaw masticating a piece of game. The afternoon was free, but the ceremonies took up again around ten in the evening, at the moment of the *grand couvert*. In the queen's large apartments, the royal couple sat in broad armchairs, surrounded by the princes and princesses of the royal family or by a few dukes and duchesses. The meal was accompanied by music, the *Symphonies for the Royal Suppers* written by Michel Lalande. At this spectacle, the royal guards allowed anybody who was properly dressed to look on, and many came from the provinces to see the king eat dinner. Louis XIV himself had called for this "free and easy access of the subjects to their prince." When the scene was in high demand, the royal family would break up into several dinners—each holding their own public meal—to the point that crowds filled the hallways of the château at dinnertime. "In the stairways one meets honest men who, after having watched the dauphine eat her soup, go to see the young princes have their porridge, only to run, breathless, to watch the princesses." Add to this zeal, the gleaming parquet and formal clothing that was as constricting as it was complicated, and you can imagine the traffic jams in the palace corridors!

Every day, the comedy began anew, growing ever more strict and ridiculous. Mastering these rules occupied minds and restricted plotting. It's hard to organize overthrowing the king when one is busy elaborating a discourse on the proper use of sedan chairs, and this orgy of futility got the better of rebellion. Frivolity was successfully invoked as an arm of repression, and the king won the internal peace of France—such a rigid regime had no problem repressing revolts. With Louis XV, protocol grew more flexible—even the king himself had grown bored of the *petit lever*—and knowing Louis XV's morals, I think it was also rather rare that he was found sleeping in his own bed. At any rate, grand festivities were probably needed, in part, to help break up the monotony of etiquette under Louis XIV.

But on that May evening of 1664, Louis XIV hadn't yet gained his crowd of sycophants—he was just a youth, "charming, young, with every heart trailing behind him," as his adored Racine put it in *Britannicus*. After the king's entrance as Roger, a troop of his comrades-in-arms followed, also disguised as characters from Arioste's *Orlando Furioso*: Ogier the Dane, Aquilant the Black,

Grifon the White, Oliver Brandimart, Dudon, Renaud, Astolfo, Zerbin, and Roland, a host of Romanesque knights embodied by the nobles of the day. The fictitious heroes were the valorous warriors of their time, and the royal display was intended to show that reality needed not blush when compared to fiction. Besides, the men were young and liked to have fun. There was a certain amount of pride and political manipulation in the *Plaisirs de l'île enchantée*, but it was just as much about the childish joy of diversion. The costumed princes paraded in a Versailles that was also in disguise—the construction work was not yet finished, so the gardens served as a natural theater set while large panels of canvas and cardboard, decorated by Carlo Vigarini to illustrate different scenes from *Orlando Furioso*, masked the incomplete château. All of Versailles had been turned into a *theatrum mundi*. Today's stones bear no trace of this past, but before becoming an emblem of French classicism, the palace was an exuberant Italian Baroque folly.

Each entrance lifted the public's admiration to greater heights—climaxing with the arrival of Apollo in his chariot. Eight feet high, it carried at its summit the god of arts and the sun, a barely disguised symbol of Louis XIV himself. Beneath his glorious patronage sat the four ages of legend: Gold, Silver, Bronze, and Iron. The float also carried figures related to the myth of Apollo: the beautiful Daphné turned into a laurel tree to escape the god's advances; Hyacinth, involuntarily killed by Apollo; Python, the guardian of the Delphic oracle; and the titan

Atlas, carrying the celestial sphere on his shoulders. Time, bearing a scythe, drove the four richly ornamented horses pulling the float. On either side, on foot, processed the twelve hours of the day and the twelve signs of the Zodiac. It made for a strange mix, with all of the mythical traditions coming together to celebrate the king. Before the stunned ladies of the court, the chariot pulled to a halt and the Bronze Age (alias Mademoiselle de Brie) had the privilege of declaiming verse in the praise of the queen and…Apollo.

After this enchanted entrance, the divertissements followed one after another. The newly completed *Tapis Vert*, or "green carpet" (the allée bordered with statues and urns that leads from the Bassin de Latone to the Bassin d'Apollon), was inaugurated with a *course de bague*. In the flaming dusk of early summer, horsemen struggled in a game of agility, attempting to capture a hanging ring on the tip of their lances. A descendant of medieval jousts, the *course de bague* reduced violence while conserving the necessary finesse, and more importantly, seduction. The men thrust their lances through rings and not their opponents' bodies, but they still competed in the name of a woman who, secretly or not, wore the colors of her champion. Which beautiful woman wore the king's colors? The most beautiful and benevolent of all, of course: nature herself. The final rays of the sunset, gold and purple, evoked the fiery helmet and golden embroidery of the royal costume, while the silver reflections of the sunset off the Grand Canal recalled the king's armor. Yet it was not Louis

XIV who won the ring. The victor's identity was cause for more one discreet smile—he was none other than the Marquis de la Vallière. The beautiful and somewhat sanctimonious Louise de la Vallière, to whom the celebrations were dedicated, must have been embarrassed by this somewhat accusing turn of fate.

Upon nightfall, the garden was lit with thousands of candles, and the seasons and signs of the zodiac set the banquet tables to the music of Lully's *Orphée de ce jour*. Dishes recalling the four seasons were served off of colored platters by more than fifty servants, led by the actress Mademoiselle Du Parc on horseback, dressed as an allegory of spring. She was accompanied by her husband as winter, riding an elephant; Thorillière on a camel, as autumn; and finally, Madeleine Béjart. Molière and Béjart, in the roles of Pan and Diana, perched on an "ingenious vehicle" in the form of a rocky outcropping that, thanks to a complicated system of artifices, seemed to float on the air. On the Grand Canal, illuminated by torchlight, there floated cardboard whales and whale calves. Each season bowed in reverence to the queen, diverting the audience's attention from the servants setting the enormous crescent-shaped banquet table for sixty, a Last Supper–like disposition that was itself also a spectacle.

> *This sumptuous meal defied description, both in its abundance and in the delicacy of the dishes served. It was one of the most beautiful things that the senses could behold. Beneath the green canopy of the garden, the night was lit*

*by an infinite number of chandeliers painted in green and*
*silver, each holding eighty candles, and two hundred white*
*wax torches held by two hundred masked characters [...]*
*which further augmented the beauty of the spot, turning*
*the round into an enchanted place.*

The first day of festivities closed with this Baroque marriage at Cana.

The second day was devoted to the Palace of Alcine. Upon the Grand Canal rocked an immense paper château representing the enchanted palace of the sorceress, moving across the waters. To amuse the queen, Roger and his knights, those glorious prisoners, decided to present a comedy in which it was shown that the imprisonment, for those who were noble and enjoyed divertissement, was a gentle one. I am not sure how aware Louis XIV was of the symbolism in this choice of subject matter, but the entire contents of the *Pleasures of the Enchanted Island* can be understood as a foreshadowing of the golden cage of Versailles. At Versailles, as in Alcine's palace, there was dancing and amusement—upon the condition of relenquishing all liberty. Roger and his companions, subjugated by Alcine's talents, were, in another sense, firmly under her control. If Louis XIV was supposed to be represented in these spectacles by the valiant Roger, he was secretly Alcine as well.

A temporary theater had been built at the end of the Allée Royale, but the weather seemed to turn against the king, with the rising winds threatening to blow out the torches and candles that lit the theater. The king triumphed, directing that protective canvas screens be erected "in so little time that the feat itself was astonishing." Beneath this ephemeral tent, the enchanted court watched *La Princesse d'Élide*, in which a cold-hearted princess rejects advances from the princes of Messène and Pyle. The prince of Ithaca is also in love with the princess, but advised by his jester, Moron, he ignores her and pretends to be smitten with her cousin instead. The plan works like a charm—love triangles are particularly effective, especially in comedy. This one ended on a cheerful note, as comedies should, with ballets and song. Molière was the author who had been chosen to make the king laugh, and it seems probable that the author had as much fun as His Majesty. A few years earlier, his *Ecole des femmes* (*The School for Wives*) and *Les précieuses ridicules* (*The Affected Ladies*) had caused a falling-out between Molière and an entire and rather influential faction of the aristocracy. *La Princess d'Élide*, however, was written in haste and was only partly in verse. Molière had the good taste, or perhaps simply not enough time, to offend anybody.

After these equestrian and theatrical entertainments, the time had come to dance. On the third and final day, as night fell, the entire court hurried to the Rond d'Eau to behold the crowning spectacle of the festivities. Everyone wore their finest clothes, for that evening there would be a ball. Upon the water, three islands emerged from the shadows of Alcine's castle, two of them featuring musicians playing violins and trumpets. The entire gardens echoed with the music of Lully. The astonishment of those assembled reached its pitch when the sorceress, incarnated by Mademoiselle Du Parc, rode astride a sea monster, accompanied by two nymphs riding whales. To the lilting rhythms popularized by Lully, a host of giants, dwarves, moors, and demons, charged by Alcine with keeping Roger imprisoned in her palace, joined together in an infernal round dance. Gigues, gavottes, passacailles, and sarabandes followed one after another at a devilish pace, with Satan leading the festivities.

Louis XIV had a great many mistresses, but none was dearer to his heart than dance. From an early age, the king devoted himself to the art, "to the point of making himself sick," as Dagneau claims in his journal. Practicing two hours every day, the king danced in more than twenty different ballets. Lully, freshly arrived from Italy, was entrusted with a French conception of Italian music that resulted in the ballet becoming an important part of French opera. This aesthetic choice stemmed from an older tradition, for dance had long played a role at the heart of French society. The French were also the first to theorize the art of ballet. Starting in the Renaissance, treatises by Michel Toulouze and Thoinot Arbeau set down a tradition that became so strong that to this day dance steps are still known by their French names.

Dance was an omnipresent activity in the France of Louis XIV—at court, of course, where dance, along with hunting and war, composed an important part of a gentleman's education, but also among the lower classes, where dancing served as a festive alternative to all-night vigils. Each region had its own particular styles, from the *bourrée* of Auvergne, to the *passepied* of Brittany, to the renowned *menuet*, a product of Poitou. The king, apart from having a restless foot, also used dance as a means of propaganda. Perhaps the centralized nature of the French state itself, of which Louis XIV was one of the initial creators, is in fact based on the steps and forms of a *rigaudon* or *gaillarde*...it's not such a crazy idea.

In his *Mémoires*, Louis XIV sets forth a veritable domestic policy in terms of dance: "All of our subjects, in general, are delighted to see that we love that which they love, that which brings them together the most effectively. Through this, we hold their heart and mind, at times, perhaps even more firmly, than through rewards and good acts."

The king, like his subjects, set about dancing. He worked on his technique with rigor and determination, not only to stage spectacles, but also to participate in them himself. It is not clear whether it was due to his reputation as a dancer or as a prince, but huge audiences crowded into the theater to admire the king dance. *Les Noces de Pélée et de Thétis*, for example, drew some thirty thousand Parisians to the hall of the Palais Petit-Bourbon. The dance craze was such that even Jesuit-run schools taught their students the minuet! The king reigned through dance, and dance was not long in ruling through the king. One of the young king's first measures was to found the Royal Dance Academy, with the mission to set down and preserve the techniques that had been previously transmitted by oral tradition.

Louis XIV also owes his best-known nickname to dance. A few weeks after the solemn entry of the new king into Paris in October 1652, the Duke de Nemours' intendant ordered up a new spectacle, *Le Ballet de la Nuit*. The program was hardly original, cramming into four evenings every mythological and popular legend that it could. It featured Venus, Endymion, werewolves, some Turks, Thétis, and an allegory of Victory. The show dragged on until the arrival of dawn incarnate. The king, in all his splendor (he was still quite young), played the role of the sun itself. This was how Louis XIV dazzled his audience in the span of a performance and became, from then on, the Sun King. (Though another story—there always seems to be one!—somewhat dampens this overly glorious account. It is said that on the night of the first performance, one of the backdrops caught fire, forcing the king to abandon his royal graces and leave the smoke-filled wings to calm the audience. The king had singed his wings after approaching the sun.)

Fire broke out on another occasion, during the ballet based on Alcine. In the sixth scene, Roger receives the ring that allows him to lift the sorceress's spell—her palace catches fire and sinks into the lake from which it first appeared. *Les Plaisirs de l'île enchantée* ended with a splendid show of fireworks. This task was left to Torelli, the man in charge of such displays. His work was a success.

> *It seemed as though the earth and water were all on fire*
> *and that the destruction of Alcine's superb palace [...]*
> *could only come about through some miracle: the height*
> *and number of the flying rockets, those that rolled along*
> *the water's edge and those that plunged into and sprang*
> *from the water created such a grand and magnificent spec-*
> *tacle that nothing could have ended the enchantments as*
> *well as such a beautiful display of pyrotechnics.*

The celebration was extended for a few days. In the following years, such parties continued at Versailles, until the king, grown weary from war and mourning, no longer felt like dancing. The flair and panache of Versailles began to fade, and memories of a Baroque Versailles with it, to the point that we have retained only the image of a classical Versailles—the rectangular, rational place of which Le Nôtre's gardens are a symbol. All of the marvelous, Romanesque decors that had once hidden the château were destined to disappear. More importantly, they had been conceived to disappear—the Baroque was fleeting.

Nonetheless, the château has continued to be a place of celebration, right up to the present day. From the night fêtes and the *Grandes eaux* set to music (when all of the fountains run at the same time), to the Nocturnal *Grandes eaux*, the year at Versailles is regularly punctuated by various public spectacles. My spring and summer are accompanied by the sound of Baroque music and the fountains of the Grande Perspective. Although the night-time water shows, where visitors meet "great" men and women of the past as they enter one bosquet or another, have brought the gardens great renown, they seem a bit silly to me. (Does this mean I've lost my childlike wonder?) I love the other evening events, particularly because they take place around the Bassin de Neptune. The setting is splendid—at the crossroads of perspectives that open upon the Orangerie and the Pièce d'eau des Suisses, I think the Bassin de Neptune is one of the places in the garden where nature and architecture are combined the most harmoniously. The convoluted shapes into which the stone has been carved—curving seashells, grimacing tritons, and sharp-tipped tridents seem to suddenly stop as they reach the calm and placid surface of the water, with the whole recalling Nicolas Poussin's famous *The Triumph of Neptune*. Every year, the water horses are replaced by very real specimens from the Grand Stables of Versailles. Built by Hardouin-Mansart, the Lesser and Greater Stables once housed the king's six hundred horses—as well as his grooms and stable boys, pages, and...musicians! Today the stables house a riding school, the Académie Équestre, which has decided to bring back the *carrousels* of days gone by, but I don't think much of these overly exuberant, modern-day pastiches. What I like most is to see animals roaming free. When I see the poor horses with their braided manes (I can imagine them standing in their stalls wearing curlers the night before), covered in feathers and brocade, tracing incomprehensible patterns on the ground with their clever hooves, I don't admire the horseman, I pity the horses. Moreover, I have doubts as to the meaning of the show itself. Under Louis XIV, everybody was familiar with horses—from the peasant who moved up in the world when he managed to acquire one, to the marquise riding sidesaddle. In those days, it must have taken a great deal of talent indeed to be cause for admiration. Today, just seeing a horse is diverting. I dislike the idea that we have come to look upon the animal the way we look upon a steam engine or a stagecoach, as an outdated object, but the people who run the school can't help any of that.

All this is to say that the reason I so like the Bassin de Neptune has nothing to do with the horse shows, but because the *bassin* is the location of one of the spectacles most often staged in the gardens, Maurice Béjart's *La Lumière des Eaux*. In June 2000, the first summer after the storm, the damage of which had initially attracted crowds of gawkers, the gardens had become as deserted as they were desolate. After six months struggling to save the domain, I was exhausted and a bit discouraged. The gardens had been saved, of course, but the sight of them at the end of June was pathetic. The boxwood was so spindly that Le Nôtre's famous "green lace" was full of snags, a certain number of paths had still not been cleared, and the allées with their numerous gaping holes just reminded me of the missing trees I had once known so well. The heavy, heady smell of summer was so absent that I wasn't sure whether it had ever existed in the first place. The convalescing park left me feeling sad and bleak, and I started thinking about leaving for my summer holiday in Oléron earlier than usual when Hubert Astier announced that that Maurice Béjart's ballet company would be coming to Versailles. The troupe would present two new ballets by Béjart himself, *L'Enfant-Roi* in the Opéra Royal and *La Lumière des Eaux* in the gardens. The project had probably been planned before the storm, but through his creations, Maurice Béjart gave a devastated Versailles the most valuable of gifts—two beautiful works of art. It was only then that I learned that the choreographer, born in 1927, had chosen his stage name in tribute to the great artists of Versailles's past, the Béjarts, and that he had long dreamed about bringing dance back to the palace. *L'Enfant-Roi* is an homage to the three great builders of Versailles, Louis XIII, Louis XIV, and Louis XV, to whom we owe the Opéra Royal. Behind these three "official" figures hides the child prodigy Mozart, who came to Versailles at the age of seven to play for the queen. Béjart's show was punctuated with texts by Molière, de Bossuet, and the diary of Louis XIV.

To my eyes, *Lumière des Eaux* is nothing less than a miracle. Before an astonished crowd of spectators, the dancers seem to move across the water itself. It would be hard to think of a more effective idea for a show—a set of the most beautiful *pas de deux* and solos from the repertoire. Certain purists might have decried such populism, but the public was captivated. Béjart's idea also had a link to history—for the wedding of Louis XIV's brother to the princess of the Palatinate in 1671, the king had decided to create a divertissement stitched together from the most beautiful moments of the works that had been presented at his theater in recent years. Molière was directed to make the choice, and he assembled fragments from *Psyché*, *Les Amants magnifiques*, *La Pastorale comique*, and the "Grande Turquerie" from the *Bourgeois Gentleman*. From his own personal favorites, Béjart chose selections of music that ranged from Mahler, Elton John, and Vivaldi, to The Residents. It was wonderful. The twilight seemed to meld with the dancers' movements, their bodies absorbing the energy of the fading day and transmitting it, in a more finite and human form, to their fascinated audience. For me, nothing else seemed to exist beyond those bodies filled with music, possessors of some strange and deep-seated archaic truth. The dancers, stage, and spectators seemed to disappear. That evening, I felt I understood the mystical imperative of dance. I wasn't alone. The 8,500 other people who attended *La Lumière des Eaux* were stunned by the choreography, forgetting the cold wind sweeping through the park and the low temperatures that were unworthy of early summer. In the words of Maurice Béjart himself, "The audience rediscovered the same pleasure the king once felt at the mixture of Turkish ceremonies, Spanish dances, and popular comedies."

SOME MODERN FÊTES have been memorable fiascos. In 1985, Versailles had the idea to try to outdo the Carnival of Venice. As in the days of Louis XIV, the festivity's organizers were not content to merely mark an event; they intended to tell a story. It didn't take long to find a subject: the exploits of the knight Roger, and the doge's gift of gondolas to Louis XIV in 1674. The black, ornate boats once again created a sort of little Venice at Versailles and marked the history of its Grand Canal. Not far away, in the Bois de Satory, there still stands a Sailors' Gate through which the gondoliers came to work every morning. Instead of a *fête de nuit*, a sound-and-light show of the sort that is a success at Versailles, told the story of Louis XIV receiving the gondolas. All of the elements needed for a successful show had been brought together: the Sun King, a nautical parade, marquises in pretty dresses, Madame de Montespan in all her splendor, and the greatness of France to make the audience dream of glory. Top it all off with the excuse of a historical underpinning, music, costumes, and fireworks, and it was the picture of a perfect sound-and-light show. Except that on the morning of the spectacle, a dense fog covered the area around the château. It was hoped that it was only a morning fog, the sort that, according to the weather report, always dissipates. But the fog grew even thicker, to the point that when night fell, one could see nothing, and the large audience found itself transported to neither Versailles nor Venice, but to a November evening in London. The gondolas passed, one after another, entirely invisible—nobody could see farther than a few feet in front of themselves. The canal seemed to make the fog over the water even denser and more opaque. Meanwhile, the audience waited patiently in the cold for the show to start, not realizing that it was already well underway. Only the actors' voices escaped from the mist—a sound-and-light show without any lights, believe me, is not good for much. The script, by Françoise de Montespan, stripped of its visual finery, felt pathetic, and the king's bravura, a sun incapable of piercing the clouds, sounded ridiculous. Even the children laughed. Then the crowd jumped at the sound of the first fireworks. A few of these managed to pierce the clouds. Suddenly, a shriek of fright broke through the rather unenthusiastic reactions. The crowd had spread out along the canal because of the fog, hoping that the mist might thin out if they just took a few steps further. A young woman had gotten too close to the area where the fireworks were set up and a rocket exploded under her feet, killing her.

I was the cause of a disaster during the summer of 2005, quite in spite of myself. At the last minute, I had been asked to come up with an activity to celebrate the unveiling of a rose that had been named "Petit Trianon." Since the rose was dedicated to Marie Antoinette, I invited the Sacchini Ensemble, named for the queen's former musician, to come perform. Sacchini had once written sonatas and operas for the queen's pleasure alone—an exclusive relationship that the court looked upon with disapproval. The Austrian queen and her Italian composer were more than simple propriety could bear. Marie Antoinette was forced to part with her musician, who returned to Paris where he died in bitter grief only a few months later. I like a good story, especially one that is sad; this is why I decided to celebrate the queen by making a discreet tribute to her abandoned but ever-faithful admirer. But the heat that day was unbearable and the music was hardly better. Under the effects of the weather, and in spite of the musicians' talent, the instruments were as loud as they were out of tune. A mournful smile crept across the face of the domain's president as he turned to shoot me a disapproving look. I understood his displeasure, but there was nothing I could do. Marie Antoinette hadn't borne such torture since the days of the Revolution. We suffered in silence. The musicians, however, looked terrified. A violinist, somewhat older than the others, seemed as though he might be on the verge of a stroke. For a moment, I had the fleeting thought that perhaps the abominable music would make people cry…This was not the case—and miraculously, the rose didn't wilt under the heat and strident sounds. A magnificent, pearly white blossom, it was far more alive than the woman we were celebrating.

Petit Trianon was actually the second rose created at Versailles. The first was an extremely beautiful, long-stemmed variety, one splendid in bouquets, that yours truly dedicated to Le Nôtre. In France, little girls are told that they are born in roses. But Le Nôtre came into the world in a most original way. In Beijing in 1998, I was attending an international flower show officially sponsored by the Chinese president, Jiang Zemin. It had been a tiring day, broken up by parades, speeches, police escorts, and polite smiles of utter incomprehension. When I finally got back to the hotel, I decided to go out and discover the nocturnal, seedy side of China. As I bellied up to the counter in a dive bar, I felt like everybody was staring at me, and I looked at the only other Westerner in the room. He was wearing beige, drinking the local beer with a frown, and looked as disconcerted as I felt.

"Are you French?" I asked.

"Bernard Durand, pleasure to meet you."

As is often the case in chance encounters (this is why I so enjoy them), we talked openly. It's easy to confide in a stranger; this is one of the reasons that psychoanalysis is such a success. We drank and, as the alcohol began to go to my head, I started talking about Le Nôtre, with the sort of professionalism that sometimes seems to take hold of me. I lamented that the great gardener of Versailles (in those days, I still admired him) didn't even have a rose named for him. In less time than it took to order another beer, my companion replied,

"I'll make you your rose."

The next day, at the flower show, I ran into my drinking buddy from the previous night at the head of a delegation sent from the major French rose nursery, Meilland. In 2000, a few months after the storm, the rose "Le Nôtre," come to life out of a chance encounter at two in the morning in a Chinese bar, was planted at Versailles.

THE BEST EVENINGS at Versailles are still those I organize for my friends. When the park is no longer on display and the château's surroundings are drained of their official ceremony, they become a place that is both simple and magical. In this blend of splendor and intimacy, I reconnect with nature and the joy of celebration. There's nothing grandiose or decadent about my own personal *Plaisirs de l'Ile enchantée*, I just try to offer my friends the best part of Versailles: its gardens. I come up with walks in the secret corners of the gardens that are ordinarily off-limits. In the summer, we have a cocktail in the Temple de l'Amour, because there's only one small step between love and friendship. Next I lead my guests to the Maison de la Reine; Pierre, Jacques, Alain, Willy, Patrick, and their wives, and Corine and I, enjoy the pleasure of an evening picnic. On the wildflower-dotted lawn that I love, we feed the ducks and tell each other stories. When we come to the cheese course, we go to the dairy in the Queen's Hamlet, the so-called Laiterie de Propreté ("the dairy of cleanliness") where Marie Antoinette is said to have enjoyed playing a shepherdess. The trompe l'œil–painted ceiling and the marble rams are the only witnesses to our jokes and memories.

We end the meal with sorbet, eaten, quite naturally, in the Pavillon Frais. When I retire, I'll have to surrender the keys to this world of which I'm well aware of just passing through, but when I do, I'll be proud to have made it echo, not with the noise and flash of society events, but instead the quiet and lasting smile of mutual friendship.

# THE RED, THE BLACK,
# AND THE PINK
≈≈≈≈≈≈≈≈≈≈≈≈≈≈≈≈≈≈≈≈≈≈

*Hardly a century has passed, and in these bosquets that
once echoed with the sound of fêtes one hears only the
cicada and the nightingale. This palace, which in itself is
like a large city, these marble staircases that seem to mount
toward the heavens, these stations, these fountains, these
woods, are now crumbling, or covered in moss, or dried
out, or cut down, and yet this former home of kings has
never seemed so pompous, so far from solitary.*[14]

THIS IS THE gloomy Versailles described by Chateaubriand,
who finishes, "When time strikes down Empires, a great name
often becomes attached to their debris and finishes by covering
them."

Still, this was not the first visit that the proud memorialist
made to Versailles. Once, in his youth, the teenaged aristocrat
had the honor of being presented to the king. He remembered
his fearful timidity upon his entry, "more dead than alive," and

---

14. François-René de Chateaubriand, *La Génie du christianisme*.

his admiration for the place. "One has seen nothing if one has not seen the great pomp of Versailles," Chateaubriand wrote in his *Mémoires d'outre-tombe*.[15]

Versailles, it is true, is quite capable of taking on funereal airs. When the château is gripped by the night, the ghosts of the past seem to remind those still living of their sad fates. An hour before sunset, the palace regains the flamboyant majesty that the daytime museum makes one forget. The gardens slowly empty out, until the moment I like best arrives—when the odd and incongruous remaining passerby is nothing but a vestige of the day's agitation. One by one the visitors disappear and the sounds of the last buses and cars fade into the distance. The gardens belong to themselves again, and they are bathed in the luxury of a sunset fit for a king, himself a fallen star. The golden light descends upon the park and is reflected off the windows of the Hall of Mirrors. The entire château seems as though it is lit up from the interior. Will there be a ball tonight? The inert mass of the palace seems, under the spell of the enchanted twilight, to call for some fête. But the chandeliers of yesteryear have been replaced by the vesperal ceremonies of the sun and the inhabitants of the park. Nobody complains of this, least of all me, when every evening, on my "rounds," I delight in a spectacle that is both familiar and extraordinary.

Suddenly, night falls and nobody remains. The animals come out. Foxes, rabbits, and owls furtively return to take hold of the

---

15. François-René de Chateaubriand, *Mémoires d'outre-tombe*, book IV, chapter 9.

territory and nocturnal Versailles slowly awakes. The stillness is magnificent. Even more than the splendid and confident radiance of dusk, I love the nighttime—silent, wild, and a bit frightening, when the long shadows of the kings and queens of our imagination pass in the dark. The gardens melt into the obscurity of night, lit only by the flashlights of the night guardsmen flickering here and there. I watch them pass from one room of the château to another, two electric will-o'-the-wisps from a dream, appearing and disappearing down the length of the allées. Something of the spirit of phantoms is here, and every evening the nocturnal reign of the royals begins anew. I don't have any interest in the supernatural, and normally, if I summon the beyond, it is in jest. Still, the charms of night at Versailles are most intense, and I rarely resist the exciting pleasure of a good fright. I have a poetic nature, not a superstitious one, and I love these specters in which I don't believe. The sculptures, whose whiteness cuts through the night, give the impression that one is being watched, while foxes furtively spy from afar. Because I see them often, I know that the ephemeral firefly-like lights that seem to disappear when one grows near are just the eyes of the animals that live in the park, watching over it at the end of the day. In the still of the night, their lives become audible. The undergrowth rustles and cracks, and the paths are animated by a dry, rapid, and regular thumping sound—that of a rabbit bolting, frightened by an unexpected arrival (most often mine) or the startling cries of night birds. In this solitary and somewhat inhuman atmosphere, I get in touch with myself; I'm on the lookout. Detached from the worries of the day, I finally feel in my element. Some flowers close for the night, and the birds put their beaks under their warm wings to sleep. Although there is movement everywhere, the impression that dominates is one of repose. I know that the park is falling asleep and that it will awake the following day, when the gates are opened and the first tourists arrive. For those not familiar with the gardens, this impenetrable quiet can become frightening.

The lack of lighting significantly adds to this astonishing sense of well-being mixed with fear. Few are the places that we spend our days that are not also lit up at night. Along highways, in villages, and inside our homes, electric light is never far away. We have lost touch with the times when the day ended with sunset. Electricity has caused the night to flee—so much so that it is rarely black. In Paris, the night sky is a reddish color, and at the seaside, at Oléron, it is brownish—without even mentioning the bright and flashy nights of certain American cities where blackouts are the exception. At Versailles, the night is a deep and unfathomable black, lit only by the green and red lights of passing airplanes or the rare and magnificent nights of meteor showers. Many of us who live in the park sleep outside on these occasions, stretched out on the lawns after having watched the spectacle of the shooting stars. I sometimes invite my friends to come watch the show from my garden, not far from the Trianon.

Another of my favorite nocturnal pastimes is my nightly encounter with an owl. The owl in question has set up house on the facade of the Petit Trianon facing the gardens, and every evening it seems to wait for me to walk past with my dog before it flies off. Although the storm of 1999 made the neighboring city lights more visible, there are still a number of spots in the park where the darkness remains complete. In these "black holes," one loses all sense of direction—and worse, one's senses no longer correspond to reality. The surprising and alarming crunch of a dead leaf underfoot has no link to the immobile nature of its reality. Everything becomes worrisome if one is a bit ignorant or dreamy. The cries of animals can be especially scary. The honest herons, comical by day, become monstrous pterodactyls by night with their strident whistling and angular silhouettes. In such a setting, it isn't long before the branches of the trees transform themselves into inhuman shadows, statues become apparitions, and the plain of Versaille, a harrowing scene from *Wuthering Heights*.

I don't believe in ghosts or any other sort of paranormal nonsense, but it is clear that the gardens are ideal for generating such fantasies. If after all of my years at Versailles I still haven't met a ghost, it seems that I am the only one. I've met any number of the living who claim to have found their way into the closed world of the spirits, and I've heard a multitude of ghost stories, some of which, I must admit, have left their mark.

In addition to multiple reincarnations of various great figures of the past, Versailles is overflowing with historical associations created under the Republican laws of 1901, in honor of the crowned and decapitated heads of the ancien régime. Every

year, the associations defending the reputation of Louis XVI and
Marie Antoinette come to celebrate the memory of their distinguished dead, and it is almost moving to see such a display
of fervor. On the day of the queen's birthday, the same group
of devotees comes and lays flowers before Marie Antoinette's
grotto. After a traditional minute of silence, one of the mem-
bers reads a speech in a voice wracked by emotion—addressing
compliments to the queen on behalf of the entire association.
The most absurd part is the contradictory mélange of admiration
and familiarity. The orator addresses her majesty, from whom he
hopes to just receive a glance "from above," as *"tu"*—and thus
reveals the assumption that the dead of high society can only be
found perched in the heights! Four or five years ago, a squirrel
had the crazy idea of running past in the middle of the oration,
and it took nothing more to persuade the group that Louis XVI,
by some obscure play of chance and metempsychosis, had been
reincarnated. When I see images of the king's heavy, weary face,
I have a great deal of difficulty imagining it transformed into the
angular, nervous lines of a squirrel…But I'm an unworthy skep-
tic, which is one of the reasons that I am never invited to this
sort of commemoration. To these gatherings can be added the
black masses celebrated by the local teenagers, who are happily
more inclined to lighting a few candles than to sacrificing virgins.
I don't mind them, as long as they don't damage the gardens.
Most of them are just funny—sometimes a bit sad—but in any
case, they show a rare devotion. I have to admit that when one

is in love, be it with a woman, a story, or a place, one rarely is in possession of all one's reason.

On one occasion, however, my reasonable, Cartesian nature abandoned me. It was midnight, and my wife had just gone upstairs to go to bed. I had a powerful urge to smoke a cigarette and felt vaguely guilty about it. Still, I decided to grant myself a few puffs out the living room window. It was snowing and I watched the Grand Trianon slowly disappear behind a white cloud as the smoke rose from my cigarette. The scene was like a snow globe, the sort of thing a tourist might buy to remember a visit. A shadow passed outside the window—it seemed to be a woman in tears, sobbing. Wrapped up in a heavy coat, her head was lowered and I couldn't make out her face. Her sobs seemed to come not from her mouth, but rather her entire body. What was she doing here, crying at my window at midnight? Was she calling for me? The few times I've seen women crying like that, they soon after attempted suicide. I turned back to the window, expecting to see a pale, accusing face pressed up against the glass, murmuring my name. But nobody was there. The snow continued to fall, swirling in the wind as it picked up. I thought of all the desperate, depressed women who had gotten through the garden gates in the night and whose husbands had called rescuers to help find them. I was sure that the woman I had just seen was about to take the plunge. I also knew that, most often, a passerby is enough to calm a person down—many suicides have been prevented by the presence of somebody else, even a stranger. It didn't take more than this thought for me to make up my mind. I went upstairs to wake my wife to tell her what I had seen and not to worry while I stepped out.

I had barely touched her shoulder when she awoke in a start and cried out in terror. She told me that she had dreamt I was standing at the top of a long flight of stairs and that a figure of death, a woman, approached from behind to push me. It was difficult to tell her that I was going to go out into the park at midnight in the middle of a snowstorm, but I reasoned with her and left the house, cell phone in hand. The ground was already covered in a few inches of snow. My car started after a few hiccups, and I set out on a nighttime round of the park. I drove slowly through the cottony, glacial silence. There were no tracks in the snow, although the snow wasn't falling quickly enough to have already covered them. I searched all of the areas in the park where one might hide and didn't find a trace of the weeping woman. My work, besides giving me an excellent knowledge of the gardens' layout, has also trained me to notice anything that seems out of the ordinary. In my mind's eye, the image of the grounds is so clear that the slightest variation catches my attention. A shadow behind a tree trunk, a damaged flowerbed, or a whisper in a bosquet is enough to put me on alert. How had the woman I had just seen evaporated into thin air?

My telephone rang. Corine, in tears, begged me to come home; this was no time to play the hero, she reasoned. The following day, everything was normal, and no sign of the desperate woman from the previous evening was to be found. Yet I remain certain that a woman in tears had come and troubled my tranquil evening.

The strangest ghost story I have heard is probably that of Miss Moberly and Miss Jourdain from August 10, 1901. On vacation in France, the Englishwomen wanted to visit Versailles. With only their Baedeker as their guide—a useless book, though considered by the English in those days as a mark of one's respectability and station in life—the two women set off for the Trianon. Charlotte Anne Elizabeth Moberly and Eleanor Frances Jourdain were both teachers, somewhat neurotic, and wore glasses, with their hair in chignons. They were politely excited to visit the former dwelling of the late queen. In spite of their Baedeker, the two bluestockings lost their way between the palace and the entrance to the Trianon. It was a little after four in the afternoon, and the day was warm and humid, leaving the women feeling stifled in the starched skirts and stiff collars of their sensible ensembles, and indignant at the forwardness of the French. Neither was accustomed to long walks, and they congratulated themselves for having chosen an overcast day to wander the long allées of Versailles, all the while wondering whether the Trianon might have a tearoom, as five o'clock was fast approaching. I know this sort of August day well, when the air becomes heavy and the covered sky seems to form a sort of hermetically sealed shell over the landscape. Such days can be somewhat disorienting: the odors of summer grow both more intense and more distressing; although out of doors, one feels trapped, as though one has been shut in by the elements. The light, white and intense due to the clouds, is particularly blinding, and a multitude of buzzing insects seems ready to feed on the smallest patch of exposed skin, the earth is dry and dusty, the lawns yellowed, the odors of certain plants become overwhelming, as does the nervous agitation of visitors gone mad from the heat. When the park grows too full, the diversity and variety of different languages turns the area around the château into a sort of Tower of Babel, a churning crowd of misery, a confusing and unpleasant mob.

But it took more than that to touch off a nervous breakdown in the English schoolteachers. They gaily chatted on the way to the Petit Trianon. Coming upon a fork in the road, Miss Jourdain leading the way and Miss Moberly following behind, they had arrived at the instant that, in literature, tends to be a turning point. From the window of a nearby building, a woman shook out a white cloth. To the surprise of her companion, Miss Jourdain chose not to ask the way from the angelic farmer's wife, but instead crossed the "broad green drive, perfectly deserted,"[16] walking determinedly down the narrower of the paths before them. The two Englishwomen had stepped "through the looking glass."

Their fate was not to have their tea with a mad hatter or to play a game of croquet fought out with pink flamingos and

---

16. C. A. E. Moberly and E. F. Jourdain, *An Adventure*, [original 1911 edition], p. 3.

an irascible Queen of Hearts, but to enter a haunted Versailles. A feeling of oppression overcame both women, who were distracted by the sight of two gardeners in green livery and wearing "small three-cornered hats." The two men held in their hands what Miss Moberly took for "a pointed spade" and Miss Jourdain a staff. At the moment of their "vision," both women took the men to be gardeners. Under Louis XV, the gardeners did indeed wear green livery, but shortly after his accession to the throne, Louis XVI asked that the staff of the Petit Trianon be dressed in the king's colors, which were ironically the blue, white, and red of the French Republic that would one day replace the monarchy. The three-cornered hat can be seen in an engraving in the Parmentier Collection showing the gardener Richard escorting the queen and the Princess Elisabeth; he is wearing just such a hat. The most troubling detail is that Richard holds a staff in his hand! The two Englishwomen claimed to have never been particularly interested in Versailles or the period in question—but in any case, it is certain that they never had access to the National Archives or the Parmentier Collection before their visit.

Both women affirmed having felt overcome by a sadness as sudden as it was oppressive and recounted that their unease only grew as the spectacle they subsequently witnessed became more interesting. Miss Jourdain asked the gardeners which path to take, and was told, with a casualness that she found displeasing, to continue straight on. As is often the case in dreams, the voices did not seem to correspond with the men's faces. The voyage in the land of the dead, according to Eleanor Jourdain, continued as follows:

> *The path pointed out to us seemed to lead away from where we imagined the Petit Trianon to be; and there was a feeling of depression and loneliness about the place. I began to feel as if I were walking in my sleep; the heavy dreaminess was oppressive. At last we came upon a path crossing ours, and saw in front of us a building consisting of some columns roofed in, and set back in the trees. Seated on the steps was a man with a heavy black cloak round his shoulders, and wearing a slouch hat.*

I know Versailles like the back of my hand, and it is not at all difficult for me to visualize the itinerary and the places described. Yet in the place described by Miss Jourdain, not far from the Temple de l'Amour, no other building exists. The Temple stands on an empty lawn, in the center of a small, artificial island. There is no structure in the spot described, but there should have been one. Maps from 1774 indicate that there were plans to build a little kiosk not far from the French Garden.

The man in the hat looked at the women without speaking a word. His skin was dark as though covered in dirt and scarred by smallpox. He didn't respond to their questions but wore a grimacing smile, preferring to stare at them with an expression described as odious, evil, and unseeing. Here, their British composure failed the ladies, and they felt terrified, only to hear footsteps approaching them from behind. A man with "a florid complexion and rather long dark hair" called to them with an "unusual" accent: "Mesdames, mesdames, you shouldn't pass this way!"

Following his advice, they changed directions and crossed a little bridge, one I know well, which leads to Marie Antoinette's grotto. In the middle of the wild grass, a woman sat drawing. She held her work at arm's length, as though to judge it, but—perhaps because of the distance or an effect of light—the page looked blank. She did not seem to hear the two women approach but was not surprised when they walked past her. She turned her head and watched them, her eyes unfocused and fearful, as though blinded by the light and unable to see them. Her face was inexpressive and not very young and she wore a large white hat atop her thick blond hair, which was arranged in a large, loose chignon. Her dress, a light summery chiffon, was draped over her shoulders and cut low across the breasts, a detail which, in spite of their fright at being trapped in a vision of the supernatural, did not fail to shock the two prudish heroines. A fichu of a transparent, green tissue seemed to decorate more than protect her neck and bosom. Neither Charlotte Moberly nor Eleanor Jourdain could claim a great knowledge of fashion, but they were nonetheless in agreement that the woman in white was quite out of style. Miss Moberly imagined she might have been a tourist wearing the traditional dress of a foreign country. Their eyes met, but Miss Moberly turned quickly away, petrified by what she saw.

Further along, a young man showed them the way and their passage through the underworld came to an end. With the same devilish smile that seemed to be on the faces of all they had met, the footman showed them back to the allée where they had originally set out, the original fork in the road. Miss Moberly complained of the gardeners who had given them such poor directions, while Miss Jourdain regretted the lack of signs showing the way through the park. The women set off and had their tea at the Hôtel des Reservoirs in the town of Versailles. Soon it was time to take the train back to Paris. They sat in silence, both exhausted, each assuming that the fatigue of the other was due to their long walk. It was only later that the women would confide to each other about what they had seen.

The "adventure" of the two Englishwomen has been much discussed since then. Their lives were changed by the success of their story, first among their friends, who encouraged them to do research, which was not long in becoming a veritable investigation. To prove that they had been witness to a phenomenon of postcognition, they scoured the French National Archives and uncovered numerous elements that corroborated their vision, as well as even more details contradicting it. One should always be wary of the facility with which one uncovers what one hopes to find...Intellectuals, scientists, psychologists, and historians all had their own explanations or arguments regarding the story, and the two women, unsurprisingly, were quite naive in accepting them. The hypotheses and polemics about their tale multiplied, but Moberly and Jourdain defended their story and their virtue to the end of their days.

The story is surely made up, but it is also troubling—and I can hardly resist the temptation to enjoy a little shudder of fright. The adventure contains too many inconsistencies and gaps, even if one does not put the sincerity of its authors in doubt. It is impossible to become lost at the Trianon, particularly on those August days when visitors abound, as they probably did in 1901 as well. Not recognizing Marie Antoinette is among the most doubtful of details—Miss Moberly insisted that she had not realized the identity of the woman drawing on the lawn until much later, during her research on Versailles. How could the women have visited the château, probably with a guide, looked at their Baedeker, and admired the paintings, all without seeing any pictures of the queen? I can understand that Marie Antoinette's spirit was aloof with them! But seriously, even if you don't pay much attention on a tour, you still take note of the stories about the king and the queen, especially when their end was as tragic as that of Louis XVI and his wife. The women's description of the queen is, in my eyes, a fraud. The authors are both capable of describing even the slightest details of the drawing woman's clothing, down to the movement of her fichu, but could not be more vague as to her physical appearance. I have a pretty good visual memory myself, but I know that if I notice the border on a person's scarf, I also note the facial features of its owner. Still, the description of the physical sensations the women experienced seems sincere.

Stiffness in the limbs, a heavy tongue, accompanied by fever, vision problems and an accelerated heartbeat——symptoms of anxiety and fear—are described by both women. I know that the gardens can seem sinister and I don't doubt that they are capable of setting off an anxiety attack. The surprising detail is that such an attack should have struck down both Miss Jourdain and her companion at the same moment. The only explanation my own reason allows me to admit would be the hallucinations of two mentally unstable women.

Still, thanks to these two Englishwomen, the Trianon has become "haunted." Eyewitness reports of the sort that often multiply on such occasions did not fail to flood in, and it seemed that Marie Antoinette appeared at regular intervals at the end of the nineteenth century. In 1870, a child saw a passing hunting party dressed in rich brocade, led by an elegant blonde woman. Don't children always tell the truth? In 1939, a young man who had gone alone to the Laiterie had a long conversation with a beautiful woman whose foreign accent he found alluring. Touched by her beauty, he asked her where she lived. The ghost of the *Autrichienne* had not lived with her parents for quite some time.

"I live in the Trianon," replied the beautiful woman.

"Will I see you again?"

"Perhaps."

Excited by this initial success, the young man relit his cigarette, which, in spite of the lack of wind, had gone out. Did he dare offer one to his femme fatale? She seemed to be ceding so willingly to his advances. But when he extended his hand to offer a cigarette to the mysterious woman, she evaporated into thin air.

In 1955, a London attorney and his wife met a woman in a yellow dress on the road to the Hamlet. She was accompanied by two men wearing hose, slippers with large silver buckles, and, of course, wigs. Miss Moberly and Miss Jourdain have had no shortage of imitators: since the 1920s and 1930s, the likes of Claire Hall, Elizabeth Hatton, and Mrs. Wilkinson, have clamored to tell their own stories of conversations with Marie Antoinette to the magazines.

I myself had the immense privilege of lunching with the queen on a number of occasions during the 1980s. The first time she was incarnated by Jane Seymour, and she introduced me to one of the most beautiful Duchesses of Polignac, Claudia Cardinale, second only to Emmanuelle Béart.

The funniest of these ghost stories is probably that of the painter René Kuder. Chosen to illustrate a book on Versailles, the elderly man was peacefully sketching near the farm. The head guard, waiting not far away, suddenly heard a shout and the sound of something falling; he ran back to find the painter lying motionless on the ground, deathly pale. When they managed to bring him back to consciousness, Kuder explained what had caused him to fall. Hearing approaching footsteps, he had left his work and turned away. Before him stood a decapitated Marie Antoinette in a gown, carrying her head, and coming down the staircase on tiptoe. The poor man. I wonder which guard had the idea to play such a prank.

I've had my own share of scares in the gardens, but each time for reasons that have been, alas, quite real. Versailles welcomes thousands of visitors every day, so it is only normal that we have our fair share of incidents. Joggers are among the most frequent of my worries. I've seen a great number of men in their fifties and sixties, who, trying to stay in shape, run themselves to exhaustion along the Grand Canal and fall to the ground with a heart attack. These occurrences are quite frequent, and the older athletes who visit my garden must wonder why I observe them with so much circumspection…We also find any number of children who have gotten separated from their group and lost their way, walking and crying for miles on end; and we find a great many elderly visitors in the depths of the park, disoriented and scared, vainly attempting to hide their confusion.

One of these stories has stayed with me. Because my office is situated in the gardens, tourists often come to ask for assistance. A while ago, a family came to ask for help—they had lost their grandfather. His daughter explained that he was sick and needed to be found quickly. His wife fixated on his appallingly distracted state, which she had put up with for fifty years. His son gestured to make it clear to me that the poor man no longer had his wits about him. Used to this sort of situation, I sent for the guards. They struck out in search of the old man, and I accompanied them, not particularly savoring the idea of waiting behind with the family of the stray patriarch. Searching high and low, we combed every area where people ordinarily get lost, but to no avail. When night fell, I started to worry. I returned to my office where the family was hiding its distress by having it out with each other. We had decided to call the police and organize an official search party when the daughter's phone rang. The grandfather wanted his dinner and said it was far too late to still be out on a walk, even for a Sunday. The senile old man, bored by the visit to the gardens, had taken advantage of his family's momentary distraction to return home on his own.

Tragically, there are also suicides in the park. From the young people who throw themselves off the terrace above the Orangerie on the night of their first breakup, to the Japanese tourist found one morning, hung upon the gate to the ballroom, people have often tried to end it all at Versailles. These tragedies are slightly tempered by the numerous, macabre plans that, luckily, don't work out. Once, in a strange mix of genres, the tragic turned comical. A woman had taken a vast quantity of pills and, groggy from their effect, treaded sluggishly toward the Grand Canal, looked around, and then jumped…into four feet of filthy water. She had forgotten that the Canal is grand indeed, but not very deep. The gardeners, hesitating between laughter and tears, intervened to save her. I was just happy to be able to bring her home alive. I also remember a pale morning when one of my crew announced, his face ashen that a woman had been found, drowned in the Bassin du Trèfle. A rescue team had been called, but I was needed to establish an official declaration. When I arrived on the scene, the usual cast of police, paramedics, and local press was already in place. The crane lowered its mechanical arm to pull the inert body from the depths of the water, where it lay face down. I turned away—I had already seen drowning victims and I hardly felt like renewing the experience. I heard the hoist lowered into the water and the voices of the men who were directing it toward the victim, when suddenly, everybody burst out laughing. A few feet above the water, clutched in the jaws of the machine, a sex doll looked back at us. Then the journalist's flashes went off, along with the temper of the police officer who had come for nothing. I felt a sudden, growing shame, followed by the recriminations of my superiors. When the police show up, there always needs to be a victim, even if it turns out to be symbolic: that time, the victim was me. On another occasion, an intense exchange between a rescue worker and a woman who wanted to jump off the Orangerie lasted several hours. The conversation continued afterwards in a café, and I am told that the victim and her rescuer became good friends.

Unfortunately, such dramas, even in the fairy-tale land of Versailles, often remain very real. One morning, when I was leaving for a meeting, I noticed a man seated at the foot of a tree. I was surprised to see somebody in the park so early in the morning—when people come so early, it's to walk, not to sit down. His appearance also surprised me: he was wearing a suit and tie, with a briefcase at his feet—hardly the accessories of an early morning walker. Four hours later, when I returned home to eat lunch, he was still there. Around two in the afternoon, I left my house again and the man still hadn't moved. I thought to myself that some people really have nothing to do and I went back to my work. But then I began to worry. This is why, at about four, I decided to loop back around to see if the mysterious man had moved. The police had surrounded the tree by the time I got there. The victim, a young man of about thirty, had shot himself.

A GREAT DEAL of blood has flowed at Versailles, much of it following the Paris Commune of 1871. While Louise Michel reigned over the barricades in Paris, the people of Versailles rose up against the Commune, which was put down after a bloody struggle. Versailles, relatively distant from Paris, was chosen as a holding area, but it wasn't easy to find a place to shut up the hundreds of communards and the even greater number of suspects. Louis XIV, the prudent aesthete, had not wanted jails to figure in the floor plan of his ideal palace. So, the large Orangerie, because of its size, was turned into a prison and became the obligatory holding area between the barracks in Satory where the military trials were held, and the nearby prisons. The odors of citrus were replaced by the acrid stench of open wounds and men forced into close confines. The prisoners were sorted and judged under the immense rotunda beneath the entryway—this area is flooded with light, but there is reason to believe the verdicts were less "enlightened." Clemenceau's witty saying about "military justice being to justice what military music is to music" is, alas, rather true. The prisoners were divided into three categories that corresponded to different areas of the building. The ordinary men were grouped together in the Grande Galerie; those who needed watching were placed back in the narrow corridors, where light rarely penetrated.

The most "dangerous" cases, the leaders, were sent beneath the stairs, where the sun never shines, in the mud and the dust. This area was nicknamed the lion pit. These men, who had, a few months earlier, raised their hopes on the barricades during the beautiful days of a Parisian springtime, were not even given space to move. It is quite harsh to deprive men of their liberty, but it is even crueler to refuse them their dignity. The communards clung to life, crowded together in the shadows, with nothing more to eat than a small ration of bread. They were given water from watering cans under the jailer's watchful eye. The prisoners were allowed to come out for a half hour every day and their exercise became a spectacle for the locals of Versailles, who came to the Parterre de Midi to observe the "dangerous classes'" suffering.

When October came, it was time to bring in the orange trees. The trees returned home, but the prisoners were carted off or executed. To this day, the walls of the Orangerie bear the marks of that bloody time. I still remember first noticing the drawings on the walls and asking a colleague who had created them. Back then, I was the same age as those young men who had died in the name of their cause a century before. For them, the Orangerie had been the place where they lost their liberty—for some, their lives; but for me, it was the place of my first days of independence. It was in the Orangerie that I began my career as a gardener. For years, I brought in the orange trees that had witnessed the deaths of the young communards. In a funny turn of fate, history had reversed the role of a particular location. The prison of 1871 had become, in 1976, a place of emancipation. Even the local characters were not without their curious similarities. I, too, at the age of nineteen, had presented myself at the Orangerie, with its ethereal forms, framed on either side by the famous Hundred Steps. I, too, knew the blinding light that causes one to lower one's eyes upon entering the rotunda, and I also had my "judge"—mine in the form of the honest Choron, who had decided my fate. I must not have inspired much confidence, because, like the dangerous criminals, I was assigned to the area beneath the stairs. As I advanced towards the spot, the light diminished until I reached the filthy corner where the prisoners were once confined, replaced by tractors. I still remember the sickening smell of gasoline and the metal lockers of the damp storage room that was supposed to serve as a changing area. In those days, Versailles still had the air of a prison. Working conditions didn't improve until the 1980s, particularly in the gardens. As gardeners, our work was hard, so it wasn't deemed useful to give us even the slightest degree of comfort. In the isolated, administrative bubble that was Versailles, we were the damned of the earth.

Some graffiti is still visible on the walls of the Orangerie—mostly names, initials, and little sketches of women. They've become familiar to me over the years: I can imagine a young soldier hastily scratching his initials before being stopped by the riding crop of some implacable adjutant; or a black-clad, bearded communard preferring to leave behind his ideas rather than his name, and trying to reason with his companion who preferred working on an homage to the beautiful Marianne he'd met on the barricades. These stories, I realize now, were similar to my own stories and those of my companions—without the tragic endings, of course. The standards of beauty weren't the same: in my day, Marianne was named Brigitte or Marina, and we called for the ousting of Giscard rather than Thiers, but the situations were somewhat similar; this is yet another reason I find the graffiti so moving. And this is also why, although I bitterly resent my trees being damaged by the knives of clumsy engravers, I don't mind so much when such activity is focused on walls.

Among the most beautiful graffiti of the Orangerie is to be found not far from the rotunda: engraved and enlaced on the damp stone, one can read the initials LPB. Although hidden by darkness and far from the main path, the autograph immediately captures one's attention. The letters are even and admirably proportioned, engraved with mastery; they seem to cry out in defiance. Beneath them, the date, 29 May 1871, is carved in the same confident hand. I took an interest in the fate of this intriguing mark's author: he turned out to be Adolphe Pigeon, born November 25, 1849, at

Sassenage, not far from Grenoble. It is a mystery how this young man ended up in Paris, but he finished among the communards, after having enrolled in the 229th federated batallion. At the end of the "Bloody Week," he was taken prisoner. Judged not dangerous, Adolphe escaped execution but was condemned to deportation on April 10, 1872, a sentence that was relaxed to three years in prison. Adolphe was alive, but deprived of his civic rights. He engraved his signature on the day of his arrest—perhaps he was afraid of dying, but his hand remained sure.

Louis XIV had decided to build the château at Versailles to protect himself from the sorts of murderous plots that he had narrowly escaped during the Fronde. His project was successful: even during the Revolution, as blood was spilled on the Place de la Concorde in Paris and elsewhere throughout France, Versailles remained safe. The king and queen only left the palace in October 1789, when the Parisians came after them, calling for the heads of "the baker, his wife, and her breadbasket." After the departure of Louis XVI, the château slowly emptied out, with courtiers either following the king to Paris, as they had done under the Regency, or, in the case of the more prudent among them, leaving the country altogether. The personnel, become useless, vacated along with them, and little by little, Versailles became a ghost town. Some curious visitors came to see the former royal dwelling, but in those troubled days, visitors were few and far between. Vagabonds set up shop in the royal apartments, and the locks on the doors were stolen, less out of revolutionary fervor than out of simple necessity. The artwork was transported to the Louvre, and abandoned furniture auctioned off, not in the Grand Trianon as Guitry's film leads one to believe, but in the grand stables. Europe's nobility, particularly the English, eagerly bought up the royal furniture. At the end of the auction, the château was completely deserted—the only affront it has known. The event had serious consequences, of course: even today, the reconstruction of the former royal collection is far from finished and is sometimes the object of dramatic and drawn-out negotiations. Still, Versailles, unlike certain pillaged churches, was preserved. Even when catastrophe seemed imminent, with the deputies of the Convention calling for the destruction of the domain, others responded that while Versailles was a symbol of absolutism, it was also the work of hundreds of France's artisans. To honor those artisans, the château ought to be preserved. Versailles was saved thanks to the latter argument. Set at a distance from the fury of Paris, as Louis XIV had intended, the palace and its grounds became a quiet and somewhat eccentric place, slouching gently into the past. It wasn't long before it became a museum.

The gardens had also been under threat, with the Convention planning to divide them up into parcels and sell them off. I've seen the map illustrating this project: the Hamlet of the Queen composing one lot and the Trianon another. Cut up in such an abberant manner, the park would have lost all its integrity and would essentially have been condemned to death. Richard, the gardener at the Trianon, averted disaster by offering to donate the harvest from the potager to the people. The Convention took little time deciding whether to divide up the land or avoid famine, and the gardens were spared. Antoine Richard was the veritable savior of the park, watching over La Quintinie's treasures, and taking a number of rare plants with him when he left Versailles to oversee the Potager du Roi. Indeed, the division of the grounds was not the only threat facing the gardens, and it is interesting to note that the revolutionaries were just as inclined to pillage the gardens as the château. Richard's stroke of genius was to have the grounds become the property of the Convention, with the king's gardens becoming the people's gardens. When a call was made to remove the royal trees from the Jardin *champêtre* to transplant them at the Museum of Natural History, Richard suggested instead that a Tree of Liberty should be planted at Versailles, making it pointless to move the other specimens from a garden that now belonged to the people. The gardens had a different status from the palace. Although people came from Paris to see the fallen luxury of the monarchy in the château and walk in the gardens, they also came to collect dandelions and mushrooms, or to find firewood, extending their paltry resources in a time of great need. The park was far more useful than the château. These were also the days of the first guided tours of the gardens for the general public.

The excesses of the Revolution often cause us to forget that it took place in a time when people were highly interested in science, following as it did the Enlightenment. The trees, particularly the exotic varieties from abroad that were a source of seeds, were carefully catalogued. Those revolutionary inventories still help us discover the history of certain specimens.

Nevertheless, the gardens would also come to know a dark period—not the September massacres, but the passage of André Thouin, the head gardener of the Museum of Natural History (and Third Estate deputy for Paris from 1789 onwards). Thouin, no doubt jealous of Richard, took out his hostility on the latter's plants. The park lost its status as a botanical garden and was methodically looted. The greenhouses, no longer maintained, fell into ruin. With Richard gone, the gardens reverted to a wild state. The Trianon was turned into an inn, the king's café was converted into a liquor store, and the old mole-hunter, Lignard, although well over the age of eighty, turned his cottage into a veritable den of vice where one could dance, drink, and gamble with the new revolutionary playing cards (where the kings' and queens' heads had been cut off and replaced by drawings of flowers and animals). The propriety, splendor, and grandeur of the past were soon forgotten, with even royal games disappearing. The bowling greens, or *boulgrin*, of yesteryear became overgrown, the terrains where the king once bowled and played croquet transforming into their modern identity as ordinary lawns. Chess, with its all-too-royal connotations, was banned, although Marie Antoinette's "life-size" matches on the black-and-white floors of the Maison de la Reine were still a recent memory. "The game of chess can teach foresight when one needs to see into the future," Benjamin Franklin is said to have observed upon visiting Versailles. Louis XVI was no doubt too absorbed in his game and had not listened. In just a few years, Versailles returned to its former status as a somewhat dangerous stopping-off point on the way to Paris, where people came to hunt and amuse themselves, far from prying eyes.

In Paris, there was no shortage of criticism concerning Versailles, with Marie Antoinette paying the price of the people's wrath. "Born with an innate inclination to pleasure, as soon as she arrived, she was seen imprudently wallowing in a state of undress on the knees of Louis XV," claimed one author of the cowardly, anonymous pamphlets. Another declared, in verse that rhymes in the original French,

> *The Court lost no time in adopting the fashion,*
> *Every woman was both lesbian and harlot*
> *One no longer had children. It seemed convenient.*
> *The . . . was replaced by the libertine finger.*

Louis XVI, the poor man, was not spared. A humorous priest, the Abbé Lapin (it remains to be determined whether he was truly a man of the church), authored a long, rhyming tirade concerning the king.

> *Everyone wonders beneath their breath,*
> *Can the king? Or can't he?*

*The sad queen has become desperate,*
*One says that he can't get it up,*
*Another that he can't get it in,*
*That his flute is sideways.*

I admit that my first reaction to these texts is to stifle my guilty, adolescent laughter, a trait that, in spite of it all, continues to haunt my character. But at heart, these salacious rumors disgust me. The worst is that such calumnies are long-lived. I think it a shame that today's popular biographies and documentaries still dedicate a couplet to the king's sexual difficulties. In the lines of the pamphlets, one can sense the rancor and libel that secular oppression once bred, but in today's documentaries, there remains nothing more than the voracious appetite for the risqué and the sordid. To my eyes, Louis XVI and Marie Antoinette were just self-conscious and had trouble adjusting to a court protocol that rendered official the slightest detail of royal sexuality. Who alive today would put up with public births or wedding nights under surveillance?

The revolutionary pamphlets underline an important characteristic of the gardens. At Versailles, pleasure and power are never distant from one another. If power is no longer present (although the château is still regularly used for official functions), pleasure has remained. The bosquets of Versailles remain a place for affection; since my arrival, I've come across more lovers and couples in the gardens than a professional detective possibly could. Is there a part of original sin that remains in the garden? Perhaps it should be recalled that the history of Versailles began with a sex scandal: Martial de Loménie, the original owner of the domain, refused to sell his land to Albert de Gondi, one of the favorites who had accompanied Catherine de Médicis from Florence. The Saint Bartholomew's Day massacre of France's Protestants also allowed for the elimination of the cumbersome landowner—faced with such powers of persuasion, his heirs found themselves obliged to sell, and Gondi became the master of the domain. The queen didn't hesitate to kill in order to satisfy her lover's caprice, and thus Versailles was founded on the scheme of an illicit couple, their vice pushing them to crime.

Although born from a sex scandal, Versailles was built on a love story. Louis XIV was, to use modern vocabulary, a lady's man. He "honored" many by sleeping with them, and he loved a few among them. It must be said that young ladies ceaselessly offered themselves to the eighteen-year-old king, to the point that the bodices of some spontaneously fell open when they spied the young heir to the throne. (Saint-Simon noted that "his Majesty never misses an occasion to roast the broom.")Who could resist a monarch? Louis XIV may have had rotten teeth and a malformed skull, but that hardly mattered. As somebody who always found it terribly difficult to attract women, I can't help but be a bit jealous! Glory attracts beauties—this is one of the great laws of seduction.

Another anecdote provides us with evidence of Louis XIV's savvy taste: A practical man, the Cardinal Mazarin brought his sisters' daughters from Italy, housing six of his nieces in the Louvre, including Marie Mancini. Marie was not known as a beauty—people at court remarked on her frizzy hair, olive skin, and skinny legs—but she was intelligent. "God, but your niece is witty," the captivated Louis XIV is supposed to have commented to his prime minister. The little Marie lived only for books—tragedies, treatises on history, and volumes on philosophy that she knew by heart. This young intellectual was astonished to discover that the future king of France knew so little of literature and the arts. A fine strategist, Louis XIV had decided to let himself be educated in order to seduce her. She spoke to him of her bedtime reading, of the novels that made her weep, the treatises that made the blood rush to her head, the music that carried her away, and the paintings that made her happy. He listened, agape, to *Madame le professeur*. Louis XIV might have better spent his time studying the history of battles and warfare, but he knew that listening to a woman was a sure means of winning her over. "Tell me about yourself," he might have murmured between two lectures. His efforts were not in vain. The pair soon joined the marvelous world of heroes depicted in the novels on courtly love that Marie so adored.

Their affair worried Mazarin. The State was clamoring for a marriage between Louis and Maria Theresa of Spain—not an Italian Maria! The two lovers had to be separated; the date of Louis's wedding had been set for the spring of 1660, according to the terms of the Treaty of the Pyrenees. Louis XIV was ordered to abandon Marie, and the monarch who would later be called absolute, obeyed his guardian. The scene of the breakup was Marie's bedchamber in the Palais Royal on June 21, 1659. Although her tears and heartbreak were not heard beyond the alcove, it is known that Racine used them as inspiration for his tragedy *Bérénice*. The king required, in spite of himself, that Marie leave Paris. The sensible Marie did not kill herself, but retired to Brouage, a little port on the Atlantic coast that has since been filled in. Brouage is not far from Oléron, and when I walk over the deserted dunes, I imagine Marie in her grief, alone and abandoned on the desolate beach that was to be her land of exile.

Although the young sovereign was hardly faithful to his first love, he clung to what she had taught him. Without her early guidance, Versailles would have never become the Italian-influenced temple of the arts that it did. Perhaps it would have remained one of the many hunting lodges built in the game-rich area, such as that of Butard, where Louis XV liked to stop off and rest after having chased peasant women and deer. The Butard is nestled in the heart of the Bois de Fausses-Reposes, "the wood of false repose." This poetic name recalls a reality that is not without a certain cruelty. The area is quite hilly, a topography that assures a good hunt; animals were led to believe they had lost their pursuers each time they made it over a rise in the terrain and lay down just at the moment when the king and his hunting party came over the crest of the hill. The prey had enjoyed false repose, and the king, easy triumph. (Hunting was not the only pleasure pursued by Louis XV when he came to the Bois de Fausses-Reposes. It is said that he also enjoyed eating strawberries off the breasts of his conquests.) The slaughter continued until 1936, with the capture of the last doe of the Bois de Boulogne. Since then, local officials have attempted reintroductions, but the area is now so encroached upon by highways that the game animals, when not killed by automobiles, hardly feel relaxed enough to reproduce.

But there is another reason, much more recent, that Butard has remained celebrated. André Le Troquer, a minister under de Gaulle, had arranged *"ballets bleus"* and *"ballets roses"* at Butard, which ended in orgies with underage girls. The most sordid detail is that, as in the days of Louis XV, the mothers themselves came to offer their children to the powerful minister. Perhaps Le Troquer had been a worthy civil servant, but de Gaulle wanted to hear nothing of it and immediately dismissed him. The affair made quite a scandal in the little world of Versailles, because the minister had obtained the keys to the hunting lodge from one of the architects charged with the preservation of the domain. Although Le Troquer was ousted, his "accomplice" was later decorated with the Légion d'honneur for "services rendered" to the state.

Ministers aren't the only ones who have frolicked at Versailles. The bosquets contain the memory of hundreds of eternal promises, and an even greater number of fleeting pleasures. Sometimes the walls still bear the traces. In the Boudoir, one of the little houses in the Queen's Hamlet, the alert tourist can still make out a graffito noting that Hélène lost her virginity to Gaston on this spot in 1912. Was it the pull of the gardens, the weight of history, or the desire to make love in the places where kings and queens once did so before? Whatever the case, the funniest and most risqué of such stories have been set in the bosquets, be it the couple caught in *flagrante delicto* by an entire busload of retirees, or the young lovers who were nearly cut short by a lawnmower they hadn't noticed approaching. Funnier yet was the voyeur, brought to me by one of the gardeners, wearing a sort of costume made of branches and grass that he had hoped would allow him to better spy upon lovers. Everybody daydreams about princes and princesses—so, when you're neither king nor queen but have a château at your disposal, it feels like the opportunity to live out a fantasy. Besides, some are turned on by the risk, and a secret shared in a park can be part of this. What a wonderful souvenir to offer to one's companion!

To budding young lovers, I offer the following advice: above all else, dress appropriately. Versailles is infested with mosquitoes, and I've seen more than one romantic idyll ruined by the impromptu arrival of a swarm of hostile insects. The destination should be the broad, green allées in the depths of the domain—the air is purer and the landscape will lend a charming country atmosphere to your lovemaking. There are also fewer passersby, and with luck, you might even see some wild animals. Boars and deer are far more romantic companions than the hordes of tourists on the Grand Canal. Above all else, these distant destinations allow you the occasion for a long walk—the distance will allow you to get to know one another better, and as the case may be, fan the flames of your companion's desires or reassure your companion of your good intentions. Admire the botanical treasures that populate these areas—the poppies, cornflowers, and autumn crocuses are just waiting for you. These are all small flowers whose beauty requires that one lie down to better observe them. The tall grasses, once flattened, will make a perfect carpet for you and your lover and will give you the excuse of being a bit clumsy. It is always warmer lying upon the grass, and you'll be hidden from view. A gentle breeze will transport you to another world, where the two of you are alone.

In my days as a single man, I used and abused the facilities offered by the park. Versailles was a real blessing to somebody like me, hardly a Don Juan. I learned, often at my own expense, that to make the ladies weak in the knees takes certain qualities. At the pool, they swoon over the lifeguard who sits, tan and muscular, inaccessible above the bathers. On the dance floor, they open their arms to the supple man who who waltzes them breathless. On the slopes, they dream of the athlete who cuts through the pack and slaloms with grace. But I am a mediocre skier, I don't like dancing, and I hate the smell of chlorine—I was cut off from the game of seduction until I discovered that I possessed an asset even more effective than the swimmer's muscles or the skier's panache: Versailles. Thanks to the gardens, I found the self-confidence that I lacked, and I was able to show off the inaccessible parts of the garden to the woman I desired. Finally, I had found a way to shine: through my knowledge of the park, by giving the object of my desire something to dream about. Some people use magic potions, others their talents, but I had Versailles.

My operations would begin early in the week. On Mondays the park is closed, and the frustrated tourists often wait in front of the gates. Among them, there was often a desperate young woman who had saved perhaps for years to come see the palace that everybody had told her about. She had finally gotten a week off from work and crossed the oceans to visit Versailles and the Trianon—to which she rushed when she understood the main château was closed! Knowing that she has planned to visit, say, the Louvre tomorrow and Chambord the day after, her hopes are dashed—she will never see the domain. This is the moment I would intervene, arriving, not incidentally, with the sacred object of power in my hands—the keys to the domain. The keys of Versailles would also be the keys to her heart. A quick exchange of glances was all it took to see whether I could approach. I offered, "just this once," to show her around. The visit would be the moment to surprise the woman with my knowledge. My words would gently lull her into the fairy-tale world of kings and queens that she has secretly been dreaming of. She might not find me handsome, but still, she might understand me to be very knowledgeable. But even more, what luck she had in meeting me! Thanks to me, she can realize her dream and, even more, feel privileged as well as gratified. Versailles is closed to the others yet entirely open to her! The pull of the forbidden fruit played an important role. Temptation and desire were in play—what will her friends say when she tells them she not only visited Versailles, like them, but that she toured it by herself, or rather, in fine company? When we come to the queen's bedroom, I would allow her to caress the silks on the bed and the superb marquetry of the dressing table, where an imposing card declared "do not touch" in several languages.

Now we find ourselves alone in the immense Gallery of Mirrors. I take her picture and she thanks me, contemplating her image reflected and multiplied in every direction. I have noticed that a certain bond forms quickly between people in such large rooms. It is easier to confide in somebody when you are alone together. I would tell her that I lived in the park and she wouldn't believe me. What a privilege to live in such an exceptional place! I would offer, to prove my good faith, that she come back to my modest abode. In other circumstances, she might have turned down my offer from prudence or prudishness, but a visit to the house of the gardener of the Trianon is an offer that is hard to refuse. (What followed, when something did follow, owed nothing to Versailles—even if it was highly agreeable.)

Time and distance make it easy to become cynical, and today, the tale of my adventures as a single man might seem deplorable. I've changed since then. And yet, I remember back then, the charm of Versailles worked as much on me as it did on the young women. It was always with a lump in my throat that I watched them leave the following morning.

Versailles has given me no small amount of pleasure and love. A few years ago, the guards and a few friends, notably Willy, the ice-cream vendor, told me about a beautiful woman who often came to the park in the company of her little girl. One day, when I was sitting in my office, I saw the ravishing woman and her daughter walk past my window. Her daughter was cute, but she was simply entrancing—I fell into admiration before the petite figure, both gentle and elegant—she wore a pair of pink shorts that took my breath away. It took nothing more to make me jump in my car and head to the spot where I knew the allées of the park would eventually lead her. We exchanged glances, and like a teenager, I complimented her on her radiant smile. Things stopped there, and I felt like an idiot. The following day, I remained at my desk, in the hope of seeing the beautiful woman in pink. She let me down—the only thing I saw was a gathering of black clouds above the gardens. The wind began to blow and as the storm approached, I lost all hope. Who would go for a walk in such weather? My disappointment deepened when the storm broke. The rain was rattling down upon the roof when, through the windows grown blurry with the force of the rain, I made out the outline of a woman hurrying under the eaves of the pavilion to take refuge from the downpour. I went outside to invite her to come into the relative protection of the entryway, when I saw who it was: shivering, soaked to the bone, and superb. The major events of my life at Versailles have always been marked by storms. In 1992, thanks to a storm, I met the woman who would become my wife. In 1999, when the park was destroyed, the ordeal made me understand that I would always be a gardener.

# MY FAVORITE SEASON

≈≈≈≈≈≈≈≈≈≈≈≈≈≈≈≈≈≈≈≈≈≈

I LOVE VERSAILLES in the autumn. Like the fireworks of bygone fêtes, the park lights up and turns a thousand wild hues. This is the most beautiful and comforting of seasons for the gardener—in winter and in summer it is necessary to protect the gardens from the cold or the heat, and the spring is a season of nonstop work that leaves one with little free time for reflection and contemplation. In the winter and the summer, I fear for my gardens, as these are the seasons of irreversible catastrophes— the storm of December 1999 and the drought of 2003 are sad proof of this. The vegetation is not at its best either; the park has too few conifers to be attractive in these seasons—too few pines and spruces to look its best at Christmastime, too few cypresses to have the allure of a Mediterranean garden. Only the orange trees manage to give the gardens a summery feel, but these are too sparse and spindly to distract one from the yellowing lawns in all the places where a watering system is absent. The park is sad in the winter. Bare and cold, it sleeps, invaded by the snow and rain. This is also the time of the year when the town feels the most present: the absence of foliage reveals the artificial light of the neighboring cities and the noise of the nearby highways becomes more audible. The animals retreat from the underbrush to hibernate and rarely venture into the gardens. Tracks in the snow sometimes mark the timid visit of some unfortunate creature, like the baby fox my wife and I once took care of. The little thing was no bigger than a bottle and covered in ticks. The animal spent the winter in our kitchen. It loved the cherry jam that Clara, my wife's daughter, fed him from her fingertips.

These urban gardens in winter make me sad, particularly since winter is the season when one has to decide which dead branches must be cut and which trees need to be removed due to sickness. The absence of foliage allows one to judge a tree's health so accurately that, by the end of November, I know which subjects won't make it through the winter. The bark grows black, hardens, and starts to flake off—a spectacle that saddens me, for it presages a coming decision I won't like to make.

From May to September, the park is taken over by tourists, and if I used to have time to rest, it was to watch the stagings of classical theater put on by the theatrical troupe of Marcelle Tassencourt. This is all the park is good for in these hottest days—a theater set. Nothing grows, nothing flowers, everything languishes and is weighed down. Much more than in autumn, nature feels as though it is withering. I voluntarily leave the formless gardens to the crowds and retreat to Oléron, where nature remains invariably beautiful year-round.

Spring usually flies past without my noticing. There is so much to be done—organizing new crews, deciding upon new plantings, supervising the orange trees coming out of the Orangerie, and bringing the parterres into harmony. I'm far too busy to see the park coming back to life. In the autumn, I finally have the time for contemplation. I watch my trees prepare themselves for the winter. Contrary to what one might believe, the autumn is a particularly active season for the world of plants, with fruits and vines coming to maturity. At Versailles the harvest is more a game than a real labor—we pick a few plums, apples, and pears in the orchards, and I have a lot of fun with the grapes that I planted in a vineyard a few years ago. In October, the gardens begin their difficult metamorphosis. The changing colors of the leaves is an extremely complex phenomenon. The sap no longer feeds all of the trees' branches and, rather, concentrates in their trunks. Deprived, the leaves grow yellow and dry up. According to the species and different factors, too complex to explain in a few lines, the green chlorophyll disappears and allows the other pigments in the leaf to appear. In other words, autumn reveals the true colors of the leaves. Many people don't realize it, but trees are red and gold. These are royal colors, and when October arrives, I marvel at the return of their reign. These are the veritable kings and queens of the park, sovereigns that no revolution could, or would want to, dethrone.

I HAVE KNOWN three different Versailles. First came the aging but terribly beautiful Versailles of my beginings. Tall, dark, and populated by majestic trees, this is the Versailles I loved—one's first loves leave an indelible mark. These unforgettable gardens disappeared on a famous evening in December 1999, leaving the suffering, devastated Versailles that I exerted so much effort to heal. This is the wounded park that needed every one of its gardeners, myself included. Today, I leave behind gardens that seem born again, and in which I find notes of grace—but not the same old charm. They will need a great deal more care, and especially much more time, before they will become beautiful. But this young park has promise, something I'm proud of. I feel a strange sensation when I see it—I know I've accomplished my mission and that the domain has been saved, but I don't feel as useful in these adolescent gardens brimming with sap. I already sense that they don't belong to me anymore. When I look back on my past, I remember the familiar faces—anonymous and famous—that marked my career at Versailles. Alas, some of them are dead now, and most of them have retired or left for other gardens—almost all of them have left the domain, in any case. One day, it will be my turn, and I won't regret it. The treasure that is Versailles shouldn't rest in the same hands for too long. I would have one last parting wish, however: to be able, on the day of my departure, to plant a tree in the memory of all the workers, earth movers, sculptors, and gardeners who have made Versailles, but who history has not deemed worthy of remembering. It would be an oak, a *Quercus robur*, a tree without pretentions, solid, and majestic, a tree felt to be common because it is found throughout France, but which, in reality, is infinitely precious. My oak, and all others like it, would be free, for the species doesn't need human intervention to prosper in our climate. May it live a thousand years and more.

**Alain Baraton** has been gardener in chief of the Park of the Palace of Versailles since 1982. He is the author of many books, all best sellers in his native France, about his life at Versailles as well as the history of the grounds. In addition to writing about gardening, he hosts popular weekly gardening programs on French radio and television. *The Gardener of Versailles* is the first of his books to be translated into English.